ALL HAT NO HORSE

COWBOY HUMOR

Willie Clement

argenta
press

© 2012 by Argenta Press
First printed in 2012 10 9 8 7 6 5 4 3 2 1
Printed in Canada

The Publisher: Argenta Press is an imprint of Dragon Hill Publishing Ltd.

Library and Archives Canada Cataloguing in Publication

Clement, Willie, 1977–
All hat, no horse / Willie Clement.

ISBN 978-0-9866546-6-4

1. Cowboys—Humor. I. Title.

PN6231.C68C54 2012   C818'.602   C2012-905837-8

Project Director: Gary Whyte
Project Editor: Kathy van Denderen
Cover Image: Front cover photo © Margo Harrison / Shutterstock; cowboy hat © Thinkstock; back cover photo © Sebastian Knight / Shutterstock

Produced with the assistance of the Government of Alberta, Alberta Multimedia Development Fund

Government of Alberta ■

PC: 1

Dedication

To my pappy, my dog Lucky and my horse Sadie

Contents

Introduction

Life is hard; it's harder if you're stupid.

–John Wayne

The life of a cowboy is one of hardship. We work long days for little pay, the work is rough, tough and dirty, and it is lonely out in the open prairies, and we would not have it any other way. However, with all those hardships, cowboys love their down time, and it is then that we get to have a few laughs.

Cowboys are some of the funniest people I have ever had the pleasure to sit by the fire with; when your days are spent trying not to get gored by some angry bull or get bucked off your horse, you need a good laugh.

So I have put together a few yucks for y'all that I hope will get a chuckle out of you. Now, cowboys aren't exactly known for their manners so a few of these jokes might be a little too blue collar for some of the younger cowpokes. In the days of the Old West, we never used words like "Native American"; an Indian was an Indian back then, and if you couldn't spell, it was "Injun." Why, just the other day I overheard a little boy say he was going to go play a game of Cattle Management Specialists and Native Americans. That just don't sound right, no matter yer political affectations.

Cowboys ain't just those dirty fellas you see in movies robbing banks and getting into fights; cowboys can be farmers, hunters, trappers and, heck, even business folk. From the great plains of Canada to the tumble-weeds of southern Texas, the cowboy's range knows no bounds. Yet as different and far ranging as we may be, us cowboys, deep down, are all the same. We are, after all, a rough-living, hard-drinking, tough-talking bunch, who every now and then like a good chuckle.

So take this here book out with you on the dusty trail, and when life is getting you down, have a few laughs with us and a lot of laughs at our expense.

Oh, and by the way, yours truly, Willie Clement Esq., has spent a few of his years out on the open range being a genuine cowboy. I have seen quite a few amazing things in my life, and so I thought I would also recount some humorous tales at the end of this book fer y'all. Some of them be true, some of them be fiction, but I assures you folks out there reading this that they will surely have you chuckling.

CHAPTER ONE

Once Upon a Time

Here are a few tall tales for you to read. I reckon y'all will chuckle a bit when reading 'em. Jokes and one-liners are great reading, but I wanted to start out with these longer stories fer those folks who like a little more meat on their bones.

The Tale of Billy the Kid's Brother

In the small, two-horse village of La Mancha, New Mexico, lived a man who kept his guns strapped to his hips, a skinny horse out in the yard and a trusty old shepherd dog that sat by his side.

The man's name was John McCarty, little brother to William Henry McCarty—also known as Billy the Kid. Now John was nothing like his brother, and that always bothered him. He grew up in the dark shadow that had attracted so much attention while the SOB was still alive, shooting up saloons and giving business to the undertakers. Billy the Kid was a bad man, but after his death, for some reason, he became a folk hero to the people of the fringes. It was a tough legacy to live with, but John embraced the notoriety.

John never had the gumption of his sibling, but he always wished that the Lord had blessed him with the quick hands and steel nerves of his brother. The outlaw cowboy life filled with danger, adventure and women became an obsession to John. He read everything he could about the cowboy way of life, staying up all night and day absorbing anything he could so that after years of nothing but high plains stories, his brain dried up to such a degree that those stories overtook his imagination. Tales of songs by campfires, fights, gun battles, high-noon showdowns, wars with the Indians, gambling, drinking, freedom and, of course, the many loose women—these all became his reality.

After some time, John started to believe that he was a genuine outlaw cowboy and that it was his life's calling to roam the open country like a lone wolf, making his own way and fighting anyone who crossed him. It was his blood right, after all, as the brother of the outlaw Billy the Kid. He even started calling himself "John the Kid" and walked around dressed in the full cowboy gear, which seemed a little ridiculous given that John was 60 years old, and that in 1937, the Wild West was no longer wild. Big cities had begun to spring up, roads were being built and families were moving in from small towns. But these developments did not matter one bit to John because he fancied himself a cowboy, and a cowboy he would be.

"John, you make sure ya got somethin' warm for those cold nights on the trail," said his 95-year-old mother before John left on his travels.

Although Billy the Kid left home at an early age and never really knew his mama, John was raised by Mrs. McCarty with the most loving and caring of hands. She felt she had failed with Billy on account of his turning criminal and all, so she doted over her youngest like an overprotective mare.

"Mom, ya ain't gots to worry about me," replied John. "I'm a growed man now. I got to make my own way in the world."

"Now don't you go doin' stupid things. I will not be known fer raisin' two devils. Your brother, God rest his soul, was possessed by evil. You are the good one. Cain and Abel you boys are. Cain and Abel," Mrs. McCarty said, holding John's face in her hands.

"Ma, yous ain't got nothing to be fearing," said John, pushing his six-shooter into his holster and tapping on the rifle secured to his horse. "I'm a cowboy now."

John then kissed his mama's cheek, mounted his horse, Jessy, and headed down the dusty paved road to seek adventure and infamy. As John was trotting down the only road out of town, people began passing him in their cars, looking strangely at this grown man dressed in cowboy gear. John, with his mind completely lost in the world of the Wild West, nodded to the passing cars with a tip of his cowboy hat and a hearty "Howdy."

John wandered on along the road with his head hung low, chewing on the end of a cigar and completely ignoring the honking cars whizzing by him. His first stop on his grand adventure was at the town general store to pick up a few supplies before carrying on.

Seeing a cowboy waltz into town was not something the townsfolk were used to except at fairs and rodeos, and the sight of one on the back of a horse carrying a rifle and wearing a six-shooter unnerved a few people. John noticed the women gathering up their young ones and scurrying off into the nearest buildings. He tried to calm their fears because as everyone knows, a true cowboy is always polite and kind to women and children.

"Pardon me, ma'am," said John with a tip of his hat, scaring a young woman who had not seen the cowboy as she exited the bank. "How do you do? I was a-wonderin' if y'all could point me in the direction of the general store."

Nervously, the young lady looked him up and down, saw the pistol strapped to his hip and with a shaking hand, pointed across the street.

"Thank you kindly!"

John then dismounted Jessy and tied him up to a post, which was in reality a parking meter, and walked over to the store. The people in the store stopped dead in their tracks when the front door opened. John took their stunned silence as a sign of respect. As he walked the aisles of the store, several pairs of eyes followed his every move. The customers' attention, though, was suddenly drawn to the front of the store when a man burst through the door and yelled, "Nobody move! Down on the floor, and hand me your wallets!"

A cowboy never hesitates, and neither did John. As the robber was preoccupied with pointing his gun at the cashier, John took the length of rope attached to his belt—because as you know, every good cowboy always has some rope on his person—and tied it into a lasso. The customers watched in astonishment as the old cowboy began twirling the rope above his head and launched the lasso toward the thief. The rope found its target, and John pounced on the unsuspecting criminal and had him hog-tied in less than 10 seconds. John stood over his catch proudly expecting the people to suddenly burst into applause, but the customers still lying on the floor were not sure what to do.

"I reckon y'all can get up now," said John.

Dumbstruck, the customers got up and began to applaud, though they were still unnerved by the six-shooter strapped to the cowboy's belt. They were so enthralled by the cowboy that they forgot about the thief tied up on the floor.

"What the hell are you?" screamed the hog-tied thief. "Is this a joke?"

"No, sir. This is how things are done in the West. If I had my way, I'd leave you gargling from a rope—heck, my brother would have dropped you with a shot the moment you walked in that door. But I think the local sheriff would love to meet ya," replied John as he gently caressed his shooter. "Now I will gather my supplies and be on my way. Shopkeep! How much for these things?"

Still with mouth agape, the cashier replied, "For you, stranger, it's on the house."

"Much obliged," said the cowboy, "and don't y'all forget to call the sheriff. Have a good day!"

And just like that, out John walked, spurs clinking behind him.

"Hey, mister!" a teenager called out. "What's your name?"

"John McCarty, but people call me the Kid."

With a sack full of supplies, John mounted his horse and trotted out of town, just missing the local sheriff.

About five miles outside the town, as the sun was just beginning to set and with the excitement of the day still playing in his head, John spotted in the distance a group of ladies standing near a series of small buildings that was actually a motel. Hoping to procure a comfortable bed on his first night out, John galloped up to the ladies and introduced himself.

"Howdy, ladies," he said. "The name is John the Kid. I was wondering if any of you lovelies could tell an honest cowboy where he might find a pillow to rest his head."

The women started laughing at once, having never heard anyone speak to them in that manner. Their laughter annoyed John for a second, but he figured that such strangely dressed ladies might not be from around these parts.

"Honey," said one of the ladies, grabbing her ample bosom. "There are plenty of pillows here for your weary head. Now, how about you get off your horse and come inside for a drink."

John dismounted his horse, tied him up to a post and followed the buxom blonde lady into the motel bar.

"It is mighty kind of you, ma'am, to show such kindness to a weary stranger," said John as they walked into the bar.

"Hey, bartender, can you fill up a bucket of water for my horse. He's been out all day and needs a good drink," said John to the bartender. "Heck, so do I."

The buxom blonde gave a knowing nod to the bartender, and he quickly rustled up a bucket of water for the horse and a whiskey (no ice) for the cowboy.

"I thank you so much, kind lady, for showing a stranger around this here lovely place," said John to the woman, whom he saw as a frontier damsel of kind and virtuous morals. "I reckon it does a lonely cowboy's heart some good to come in off the trail and see such a welcoming, pretty face, if you permit me to say."

Not accustomed to being spoken to that way by men, the woman took a shining to the polite cowboy and decided to play along in his little delusion. After all, it was a slow day.

"Why, it is mighty kind of you, sir. We don't get many gentleman around these here parts," she said.

"Excuse me, where are my manners!" said the cowboy. "My name is John the Kid. What angelic name did the Lord bestow upon you?"

"You may call me Roxanne."

"Pleasure to meet you, Roxanne," replied John, removing his hat and slightly bowing his head. "So what's a pretty lady like yourself doing in these parts? You ought to be wined and dined in some big city."

"Why, I do declare!" said Roxanne, blushing for the first time in years. "Stranger, you might look a little odd, but you sure do know how to charm a lady."

"Just acting right, is all," said John, blushing a little in the face.

They sat drinking and talking for a few minutes. Roxanne gently flirted with the old cowboy, something she hadn't done honestly in years. Rubbing his inner thigh, she whispered in his ear, "How 'bout we go out back. I got a room there where we can have a little more privacy. And don't worry, Sugar, this one's on the house."

John thought she was offering more whiskey and gladly followed the lady to a back room, hardly able to believe that his cowboy adventure was getting off to such a good start.

The moment the door was shut behind them, Roxanne pounced on John, tearing off his shirt and kissing his neck. She was just about to get his pants off when the door was kicked open and a large man burst into the room, cussing up a storm and making wild gestures before John could even get his pants buckled back up.

"You bloody whore!" screamed the burly man. "How many times have I told you to get the money up front!"

"Buuutttt Rocky, hun…" was all she managed to say before receiving a vicious slap to the face that sent her to the floor in a whimpering heap.

"This is your last warning, whore!" he screamed down at her. "And as for you, Cowboy! You gots to pay for her services now, or else."

John did not answer the crazed brute; instead, he slowly put his shirt back on and placed his cowboy hat on his head.

"Well, did you not hear me, loser! I said, pay up!"

John slowly lifted his head, stared at the man and said in a low, gruff voice, "You shouldn't have done that."

The man threw his head back and let out the most awful spine-chilling laugh. This moment of inattention gave John the opportunity he needed. In a flash, he leapt across the bed and landed a hard right fist to the man's jaw, laying him out cold.

"Nobody talks that way to a lady," said the cowboy, who then spit in the man's face. "You gonna do something or just lie there and bleed? Nothing, I guess. Miss Roxanne, are you okay?"

The woman could hardly believe what had just happened, and she stared up at the cowboy like she had seen the face of an angel. "I can't believe…You just… He's out. Where did you come from? They sure as hell don't make 'em like you anymore."

"I don't know who that man is or what that nonsense was about, but I do know that he dun messed with the wrong cowboy," said John, straightening his hat. "Roxanne, I reckon we should mosey on out of here before this thug wakes up."

"I would say so, but where are you going?" asked Roxanne, hoping that he had room on his horse for her.

"Why, I'm headed back out on the trail. Freedom is my life, and I jus' sees where it will take me," he replied, gathering up his belongings and heading back out to see about his horse.

Roxanne followed him outside.

"John," she said breathlessly, "take me out of this place. Take me with you."

"Roxanne," he said, caressing her cheek, "the open trail is no place for a lady as delicate and of such high morals as yourself. Take these silver dollars and buy yourself a ticket to the big city where a girl like you will be treated right." John then kissed her full waiting lips, wiped a tear from her face and mounted his horse.

"Will I ever see you again?" she asked.

"Maybe some day our paths will cross, but until then, I must go where destiny calls," he said, and with that he rode off into the setting sun, leaving Roxanne on the side of the road scratching her head, wondering what the hell had just happened.

With the light quickly dying, John rode off into the night. He traveled for about an hour before the darkness completely swallowed his sight.

"Looks like we need us a place to rest for the night, Jessy," John said to his horse. The city lights had faded out completely, and nothing but open land and stars were in front of him. "Ain't this the life, Jessy. I ain't got nobody telling me what to do or where I can go."

As he galloped through the darkness, he began to sing.

"Oh, give me a home,
Where the buffalo roam,
Where the deer and the antelope play.
Where seldom is heard a discouraging word,
And the skies are not cloudy all day!"

Seemingly out in the middle of nowhere, John found a nice spot under a tree to rest for the night. After tying up Jessy, he gathered up some wood scraps, built a small fire and laid out on his blanket, staring up at the stars.

"This is the life, eh, Jessy. No cares, no worries, nothing but time and the world before us. Well, good night, I suppose."

The next morning at the crack of dawn, John was up, saddled and back on the dusty trail, just missing the homeowner who went outside to fetch his newspaper but found a pile of horse manure, a charred fire pit on his green lawn and his wood pile scattered about.

Out on the trail, John was enjoying the early morning sun on the back of Jessy. With the city far behind him, he could relax and enjoy the peace and quiet.

Despite not having a bad bone in his body, John thought that in order to reach the same level of infamy as his brother, he would need to toughen up a bit. Sure, he had lassoed a thief and punched out an abuser, but these were all good deeds. His brother was a no-good, hard-drinking bastard who would shoot a man in the face for looking at him cross-eyed. John didn't know if this was true or not, but he even heard that his brother shot a man dead while playing poker because he suspected him of cheating. No one remembers the heroes of the Wild West. The heroes are the bad guys, the outlaws, the men who had no masters. John needed to be his own master.

Out in the middle of nowhere, though, John had no idea what bad deed he could possibly do. Then he heard it. Off in the distance, behind a row of trees, a train chugged along the tracks. He had read countless tales of cowboy bandits pulling up beside trains and robbing the passengers. John knew he didn't have the nerve to kill a man, so a heist would be his ticket to infamy; it had to be.

Changing course, John followed the tracks to a small railroad station that had just a few people milling about. The train he had heard had already passed, so he wondered if he had missed his chance because, to his mind, trains only passed through once a month or even longer intervals. His train-robbing days were not getting off to a good start, but he heard the distant sound of a train whistle, and people started to gather on the platform. He thought they were dressed a little strangely for a train trip—the men wore fancy suits that some New Yorker would wear, and none of the women had any parasols to keep the sun off them or had any male escorts.

When the train pulled into the station, the passengers got on, and John prepared his horse for the adventure. The key to a successful train robbery is to do your thievery when the train is between stations; it made your getaway easier. So the moment the train began to pull away, John dug his heels into Jessy's sides and started the chase.

But right from the get-go, things did not go as he had hoped. He had seen and heard that trains were slow enough for a good horse to keep up, but Jessy couldn't keep up with this train that kept going faster. John did his best to stay with the train, but Jessy was tiring.

The passengers on the train were just settling into their seats when some of them happened to look out the window and saw a strange man dressed as a cowboy chasing the train. For some strange reason, no one thought anything of it, and they continued to read their newspapers or carry on their conversations.

Meanwhile, John was about to lose the train, so he stood up on Jessy's back and made a desperate leap for the last car. He just made it onto the platform, and when he looked back at Jessy, he realized he had not planned on how to get off the train.

John opened the doors to the train car, and all the passengers turned their heads. John had no idea what to do, so he simply sat down in one of the empty seats. Sitting across from him was one of those unescorted women.

"Howdy, ma'am," John said nervously.

"Hi," she said, looking over John with a curious eye.

His mind raced, trying to figure out what to do next. "Umm, ma'am, umm, could you tell me where this train is headed?"

"Sir," she said with a confused look on her face, "we are going to Las Vegas."

John had heard of the place, but to him it was a small mining town. He thought maybe he could make his name in that town.

Sitting back in his seat, John looked out the window and was a little taken aback by the speed of the train, and he began to sweat. The woman across from him slowly realized that the cowboy was of no real harm and laughed to herself at his discomfort.

John continued to look out the window and watched the world speed by, and within 20 minutes of sitting down, he was fast asleep.

Several hours later, he woke up as the train came to a halt at the station in Vegas. But what was once a small, dusty mining town and a stop on the way to California had quickly turned into the gambling capital of the United States. John could not understand what he was seeing because to his mind, it was still 1837 not 1937.

He got off the train and walked through the city, and for the first time since he left his house, he began to see the world for what it really was. Cars replaced horses on the street, people were dressed differently than he was and the buildings were taller than just one-story wood shacks.

Las Vegas was a town of bright lights, big buildings and thousands of fancily dressed people who talked fast and moved even faster. The strange thing was that nobody looked at him. He was just another performer to them, working for the new casinos.

John, however, did not want to believe his eyes. He saw the cars and the people, but in his mind, he twisted and rearranged the images until they fit his reality. Now more than ever he was determined to make a name for himself.

John walked into the nearest casino, pulled out his six-shooter and yelled, "Everybody down on the ground. This is a stickup!" It took mere seconds before he was tackled by 10 security guards and tied up like a baby steer.

For John, his capture spelled the end of his cowboy career. After being handcuffed by the security guards, he was carted off to the police station and thrown in jail. Instead of keeping him in prison, however, the state of Nevada decided that John was obviously insane and should be put in an institution.

So thus ended the great journey of the poor cowboy hero. He spent the rest of his days walking around the grounds of the institution, mutterings things about Jessy and Billy the Kid. And whenever a nurse or another patient approached him, he would put his right hand to his waist and do a pretend draw on the person with his finger gun.

The New Cowhand

The early days of running cattle were tough, but the good company on the trails and the good grub helped make the journey go easier. The cowboy life, though, had a way of chewing up and spitting out the weak ones, and every once in a while, a rookie cowhand joined us regulars on the cattle rush. Being out in open country with a new fella was not always easy. Us older cowboys are set in our ways, and we sometimes went out of our way to make the rookie's job a little harder, but it was all in good fun.

I recall one young cowhand who just did not seem to understand the cowboy way. He was what we called a chronic grumbler. He complained about everything, from his horse to the smell of the wind, but his favorite target for his sass-mouth was the camp cook and his food.

Wanting to keep harmony on the trail, we older cowboys kept our mouths shut, but this cowhand was not learning, and he talked so much and so fast that we swear we could smell sulfur. His constant chattering was getting to a few of the fellas, so being the senior cowboy on the job, I pulled the young mule aside and had a talk with him. He went on and on about this and that, but his main gripe was the food. I told him that what he needed was a "liver regulator." Naturally, he did not know what that was, so I told him that the cook might be able to provide him with some of that unique medicine he kept in the grub box. The other cowboys completely agreed with my assessment and sent him off to see the cook.

That night at meal time, the green cowhand was at it again, talking and complaining his way through his supper. The moment he finished his meal, he gets up and walks over to the cook. We boys were all laughing underneath our Stetsons.

He says, "Say, there, how 'bout some of that liver regulator they's been telling me about? I hope it's better than the food we's been eatin' so far."

The grizzled old cook looks the greenhorn over with an evil eye and a devilish smile and says, "It sure is, pardner." The cook then reaches into the old grub box, pulls out his pistol and cocks the hammer.

The cook then says, "This is the best damned liver regulator I know about. An' if I hear one more gripe out of you, yous for sure gonna get a big dose."

We all burst out laughing. The cowhand did not say much after that incident, and once the cattle haul was up, we never did see him again. I hope he took that lesson with him wherever he went.

Life in the Wild West

Say, "The Wild West," and every person will get an image of tough men, living free and dying young. They think of a place of gambling, loose ladies, gunfights, drunks and cattle, cattle and more cattle. They would be right. The frontier attracted people without a place to call home, people with great ambitions, people running away from some other life, people with criminal pasts, all thrown together into a landscape of extremes, without law or order. The West truly was wild.

To survive in such places, you had to be tough, but not every cowboy was as tough as he put on. There were a lot of braggarts in the Old West. There was this one braggart in particular who loved to walk around town and show off his gun skills to everyone he could. He would flip his gun into the air, twirl it on his finger and shoot bull's eyes from a distance. Problem was that the young greenhorn was so full of himself that he did not pay enough attention to what he was doing, and one day while twirling his gun, he let off two shots that killed two innocent people.

While a local judge deemed it accidental, one day, that same young greenhorn disappeared from town and was found three days later hanging from a tree. The executioners left a note on his body that read, "This is no accident."

Being a tough cowboy is not about how good you twirl your gun or how fast your horse is, but some fellas just plum did not get it.

There was another case of a braggart that I can recall in New Mexico. This cowboy egged on copious amounts of "bravemaker," jumped on his horse and rode through town like a fool, firing off his gun and hollering worse than a jackal caught in a trap. Then the foolish cowboy walked into the saloon and disrupted everyone's evening by shooting off his gun and carrying on about how he was the meanest SOB in all of the south and how he picks his teeth with his Colt .45. The fool was got so drunk that he even said he used a cactus for a pillow. The folks in the saloon had seen this all before and continued on with their business. The fool, though, kept screaming, "I am a wolf! I am a wolf!"

Finally, one mean-looking hombre stood up, walked up to the braggart, puffed out his chest and started fixing his pistols. "So, you're a wolf, huh?" the cowboy said. "Jes' what sort of wolf are you?"

Confronted with a man twice his size and with a face that had probably seen a few men die, the braggart slumped his shoulders and whimpered, "I'm jes' a little coyote." Well, the braggart did not have anything else to say so he turned tail and ran out of the saloon.

That also reminds me of another story I heard out of San Antonio. A stranger rode into town and started jawing about how he was the toughest, meanest gunslinger in all of Texas and the West. He would not stop flapping about how he had killed some poor soul in Austin or put three Mexicans into the grave in Nevada.

In the saloon, he challenged any man to a duel, but the townsfolk of San Antonio knew better than to pay any mind to a braggart. It wasn't until he began jawing on about old Reg Wayne that he got everyone's attention.

"That's right," said the stupid braggart. "I comes here to shoot up the infamous Reg Wayne. I ain't afraid a-nuthin'. Why, if that varmint was here, I'd put a piece of lead right between his eyes."

It was then that someone came through the door and hollered, "Howdy!" to the barroom, to which someone called back, "Howdy, Reg Wayne! We'uz just talkin' about you."

The stranger suddenly went stiff as a board and began to sweat. "Umm, I, umm, I thought you wus in Wyoming, Reg!" And then without pause, the stranger launched himself out the window, jumped on his horse and took off.

"What was that about?" asked the man who walked into the bar.

"Ah, nuthin', Vic, that was just the way we deal with braggarts around here."

Where was the law in all this, you might ask? Well, the West had a strange relationship with law and order as it was at the time. It was something that could be doled out by a sheriff—as long as his six-shooter was fast enough—a supreme court judge or even by some backwater toothless cowboy with a noose and a cottonwood tree.

Justice for most was just common sense. If you done a fella wrong, you paid the price; it was easy to understand and easy to enforce. If someone killed a man, well, then it was reasonable to everyone that the man should be killed. This down-home justice suited folks just fine; for example, I can recall the case of one horse thief and murderer, a Mexican named Tuco.

For weeks Tuco had terrorized a little border town in Texas, stealing people's horses and killing anyone who tried to stop him. Now it was left up to the local sheriff to deal with the outlaw, but it just so happened that the sheriff was a little slow and not so eager to get himself shot up by Tuco, seeing as the thief had already gone and killed a few able-bodied men. The town couldn't continue on in such a manner, so several of the men got together and set up a trap to catch Tuco.

One day a big show was made in town that a local farmer had just bought 'bout five or six new horses. They were paraded through town, so that Tuco would know without a doubt that he had something new to steal. That night, several men laid in ambush around the farmer's barn.

Sho' 'nough, Tuco showed up and was caught red-handed. Seeing as the sheriff was a little weak in the knees, Tuco was found guilty by the vigilante and taken out into the desert and strung up by his neck.

Vigilante justice was illegal, but the vigilantes visited with the local coroner (as well as the local undertaker) and asked him if he would be so kind as to square things in his report so as good people wouldn't get punished for killing a bad man.

"Well, I'm not so sure I can do that, boys," the coroner answered. "Did you leave Tuco up in the tree all night?"

"Yes, sir, we did."

"In that case, ole Tuco surely would have froze to death if he hadn't busted his neck. I reckon I'll just put down in the report that he died from 'overexposure.'"

In the West, justice always came to those who deserved it.

Deserving to die was one thing, but sometimes being stupid was another reason that got men killed and a look in the other direction from the lawmen.

There once was this cowboy out in Oklahoma who was sitting in a saloon and got to arguing with a trapper over something that only matters to a drunk. Well, things got heated between the two, and the trapper settled the argument with his pistol. The coroner of that little town did not need to call in the sheriff as he put down in his report, "Anyone dumb enough to call a long-haired, bearded, whiskey-drinking trapper a bunch of names he would not want his momma to hear had, in the most strongest of sense, died of ignorance."

Life, though, was not all doom and gloom out on the open plains and cattle ranches. If there is one thing a cowboy is known for, it's how to have a good time. As they used to say, "Laugh kills lonesome."

Seeing as there were not many of the ladies around to keep them boys in their places, the best way to pass the time was to play pranks on each other, and the favorite target for the prankster cowboy was someone on the job who was not pulling his weight.

I can remember this one time out on the range, we wus working with this new fellow named Cotton Smith. The cowpoke was as tall as a cottonwood tree and about as fat as a buffalo. At first, we all thought the big boy would be perfect for chucking hay, but more often than not we found the lazy SOB sleeping on top of the hay instead. If there is one rule when working the range, it's that you must work your fair share. After some time of sleeping his way through the days, the boys and I decided something had to be done about ole Cotton Smith.

Our last shred of patience with Cotton came one particularly hot and busy day, when we found the old snake curled up on a haystack, with his boots off, sound asleep. I got one of the boys to find and kill the biggest dang tarantula you ever did see. We then placed the dead spider next to Cotton's butt. We then tied a pin on the end of a long stick and jabbed the sleeping beauty in the rear a couple of times until he woke up in a fright.

As we tried to hold back our laughter, one of the cowboys rushed over and pretended to squish the spider with his boot. Well, Cotton took one long look at the squished tarantula and turned all shades of white. Immediately, Cotton began dry heaving.

The other cowhands added fuel to the fire by telling him all sorts of horrible deaths they had seen on account of tarantula bites. My favorite was the story of a feller whose pecker fell off after getting bit. Wasn't true in the least, but that sho' did scare the hell out of Cotton so much he thought his rear-end might fall off. Then one of the boys said that his father was a doctor and that he knew an ancient remedy that the Injuns used.

First, the prankster poured a pint of castor oil down Cotton's throat, and he immediately began tossing his lunch all over the place. Cotton was then told to follow that up with a cup of vinegar, some warm water that I believe had my socks soaking in them, some hot whiskey, and finally, a whole jalapeno pepper.

Well, poor old Cotton was certain the medicine was worse than the tarantula poison, but after some time spent with things shooting out both ends, Cotton was feeling okay and was thanking us for saving his life.

We never did tell Cotton that we had tricked him; we didn't have to because the poor boy was afraid of lying down on the job and especially on those haystacks.

Life in the West was not always wild, however. There was, after all, a softer side to the cowboy. Though it must be said that no matter how much soap, water and scrubbing a cowboy did after a hard day's work, it did little to clean up his lack of social graces in the presence of women.

This was not the fault of the cowboys as they was not really exposed much to the ladies. The West was filled with men, but there was very few women folk, making for many awkward encounters.

The idea that the cowboy of the Old West was this romantic figure is the result of Hollywood movies. For the most part, cowboys spent a good deal of their day surrounded by other men, and when a lady happened by, many of them didn't know how to act. There were a few John Waynes out in the West, but we was just a bunch of clueless men trying our best to impress the fairer sex.

I am reminded of an old friend of mine who took to fancying a lovely widow. She had this young son that the cowboy took a shining to, giving the lad piggyback rides and spending a lot of his free time with him. A friend of his asked him why he was going to such lengths with the boy.

"Why, I been a cowhand fer most of my life, and I know that when you pull along the calf, the old cow will surely follow."

Finding a girl was one thing, but snagging a pretty one was dang near impossible. When one little lass came from down east, well, all them cowboys went wild for this beautiful vision and tried to win her affections in the only way they knew how.

When Miss Sally Long arrived on her father's Texas ranch, the battle for her hand began between the young men of the town. It was a fierce rivalry between the young cowpokes, but one of them thought he got the upper hand when he came up with the brilliant idea of taking a little calf and branding a charred "Sally" onto its hindquarters. Well, the other boys thought this a good idea too and branded various messages into the other poor calves. One cowpoke even went as far as inscribing a poem on one calf:

"Roses are red.

Violets are blue.

Sugar is sweet,

And so are you."

Let's just say the sight of so many charred and branded calves on her front door every morning frightened the genteel lady unaccustomed to receiving such lively gifts from suitors. She was in such a fret over what to do that she sent a letter back to another suitor in the East and agreed to marry him. Well, that young man was on the next train out, and when he arrived, those cowboys were forced to ride off with their gifts. Imagine how those poor cowboys were left red-faced riding through town with love notes burned into calves that they would have to raise for years to come.

If a cowboy were lucky enough to snag a woman, he did his best to protect her from other suitors. This made the average cowboy a rather jealous type of person. The worst case of blind jealousy I ever did hear about was the story about Roy.

Roy was an honest cowboy who went to church every Sunday and was a firm believer in the vows he and his young wife had shared. But his wife was rather young, and after a few years of marriage and living out in the middle of the Texas plains, she wanted to get out of the backcountry and see a big city. So she traveled for days and finally reached the place she had always dreamed about.

Missing her husband dearly, she wrote him a letter telling him of all the wondrous things and modern technology. She wrote of the magnificent shops and the buildings as high as mountains, but the most amazing thing of all for her was having a hotel room with running water. A short time later, she received a wire from her cowboy husband that read:

"Get rid of that Indian in your room or our marriage is over!"

Life sure was tough out in the Wild West, but cowboys didn't expect much. It was a life that they embraced because it gave them freedom—they certainly weren't in the profession, as it were, for the money. Often, a cowboy had nothing more than a horse, a saddle, a six-shooter, a change of clothes and a blanket, and for most this was enough. The Old West was the home of the poor man, and the primary reward was just being a free-living cowboy.

These meager possessions, though, were everything to the cowboy. I can recall a dear friend of mine who was moving a herd of cattle when something spooked the animals and sent his packhorse running off. Well, that boy dun freaked out and ran after the horse, screaming, "Someone stop that mule—he's got my lifesavings!"

Actual money was a luxury for a cowboy, and when payday came around, that money was used for gambling, booze and women. I can remember myself getting paid on a Friday and coming back to work the next day with not even a red cent. But dang those were good nights!

Seeing as money was often scarce, some of the cowboys sought out other means of getting their hands on cold hard cash. Bank raids, train holdups and stagecoach robberies were sometimes done out of greed, and sometimes the boys liked to see themselves in the Robin Hood spirit.

Another good friend of mine was robbing a train one afternoon when he came across an old gentleman sitting quietly on the train.

"Put yer money in the sack," said the robber.

"I'm sorry, but I have nothing to give," said the man.

"How come? Who are ya anyway?" demanded the robber.

"My name is Reverend Burnett. I am a Catholic minister."

The train robber took a step back, looked over the older gentleman then dropped a large sack filled with money in the minister's lap.

"Here," said the thief. "You take this and give it to someone who needs it. I'm a Catholic too."

Committing robbery sometimes was done simply for sport. John Curley once walked into a church and used his pistol to force the congregation to sing his favorite hymns for a few hours before he passed the collection plate around and took up the largest donation in church history.

Yet despite the occasional moment of violence, the Old West was an open-door landscape that offered true freedom to those who sought it and honored the values of hospitality, respect and a good sense of humor. Without those values to fall back on, life in the Wild West would have been miserable for a cowboy.

Animal Tales

Think Before Speaking

A cowboy buys a beautiful new horse. The salesman tells him that the horse's former owner was a famous preacher.

"This horse is very religious," says the salesman. "And he only responds to special commands. For example, instead of saying 'Giddy-up,' you have to say 'Praise the Lord.' And instead of telling him to 'Whoa!' you gotta say 'Hallelujah!' Got that?"

"Praise the Lord and Hallelujah," says the cowboy as he nods.

Weeks later, the cowboy is riding through unfamiliar territory. Gorges and cliffs fall hundreds of feet on either side of the trail. The cowboy wants to stop and take a rest, but he confuses the two commands the salesman had taught him.

Q: What do you call a horse that lives next door?

A: A neigh-bor!

"Praise the Lord," the cowboy says, but the horse keeps on galloping faster and faster. The cowboy sees that the trail up ahead ends in a dangerous cliff.

He tugs and pulls at the reins even harder and yells, "Praise the Lord! Praise the Lord!" but the horse continues to race toward the cliff.

All at once, the cowboy remembers the right word.

"Hallelujah!" he cries.

The horse immediately stops, mere inches from the crumbling edge of the cliff.

The cowboy breathes a sigh of relief, pulls off his hat and wipes the sweat from his brow. "Praise the Lord," he says.

Cowgirl Face Palm

Two blonde cowgirls each buy a horse and keep them in the same stable. Since the horses look so much alike, the two women discuss how they will tell the horses apart.

"I have a great idea," says one blonde cowgirl to the other. "Just so we don't make a mistake and take the wrong horse, you can have the black one and I will have the white one."

"You're so smart!" says the other blonde.

Bartender

A cowboy walks into a bar and sees a cow serving drinks behind the counter.

"What are you staring at?" asks the cow. "Never seen a cow serve drinks before?"

"It's not that," replies the cowboy. "I just never thought the horse would sell the place."

City Slickers

With dreams of rodeo glory dancing in his head, a tenderfoot decides to hone his horsemanship. He mounts his horse, and it springs into motion. The horse gallops along at a steady and rhythmic pace, but the tenderfoot begins to slip from the saddle.

Terrified, he grabs for the horse's mane, but he can't seem to get a firm grip. He tries to throw his arms around the horse's neck and almost loses his balance. The horse keeps galloping along, seemingly impervious to its slipping rider.

Finally, the tenderfoot tries to throw himself to safety by leaping from the horse. Unfortunately, his foot gets entangled in the stirrup, putting him at the mercy of the pounding hooves of the horse. His head is battered repeatedly against the ground, and he is moments away from unconsciousness when, to his great relief, the Walmart manager runs out and unplugs the horse.

Q: Did you hear about the cowboy dressed in brown paper?

A: He was arrested for rustling.

Horse in Bar

A white horse walks into a saloon and orders a pint of beer.

"Wow," says the bartender. "We sell a whiskey named after you."

"What, a whiskey named Eric?" says the horse.

Smart Horse

John is buying a horse from Hank.

"And is he well bred?" John asks Hank.

"I'll say he's well bred," replies Hank. "In fact, he's so well bred that if he could talk, I doubt he'd speak to either of us."

Really Smart Horse

A cowboy is riding his horse one day when he accidentally gets thrown off. The quick-thinking horse pulls the cowboy to a shady oasis, props him up against a tree and then gallops off for help. The horse soon returns with some folks from a neighboring town, one of whom is a doctor. The doctor and the others bring the cowboy into town and nurse him back to full health.

A week later, when the cowboy is telling the story to his buddies at the saloon, one of them says, "That's the gol-dang smartest horse I ever heard tell of."

"Aw, he ain't that smart," says the cowboy. "The doctor he brung with him was a vet."

Really, Really, Smart Horse

A group of old cowboys are sitting around arguing, since there's not much else to do that afternoon. One old-timer starts talking about how he has the smartest dog in all the world. He tells the cowboys that his dog was once caught in a wolf snare by the tail.

"Can ya guess what he did then?" the old-timer asks.

"I bet old yeller bit off his tail!" says one cowboy, laughing.

"No, ya crazy!" replies the cowboy.

"I bet ya he pulled up the stake and dragged it back to you," says another cowboy.

"Nah, he jes' started up a howl and kept it up till I comes round and took the trap off his tail."

"Bah, that ain't smart," chimes in another cowboy who had been silent up until then. "I reckon I've never owned a smart dog, but I sure as heck had the dumbest dang hoss that walked this earth. I'll tell ya what that critter dun did one time when I drank too much cactus juice and passed out drunker than a hillbilly at a rooster fight. Well, that dang hoss picked me up and threw me over his back and carried me some 20 miles to the ranch. Then the critter tossed me into my bunk, pulled off my boots with his teeth and even managed to tuck me in. And I swears I think he kissed me goodnight. The dumb hoss then went into the kitchen, fixed up a pot of coffee and brung me up a steaming cup with cream and sugar. Seeing as I couldn't work the next day, my hoss then corralled the cattle all by hisself so the foreman would let me sleep it off. When I woke up the next day and found out what that varmint had been up to, I cussed the stupid hoss out fer two days and then sent him off into the wild with a good-riddance boot to his rear-end."

Q: Why couldn't the pony talk?

A: He was a little horse.

"What the heck!" says one of the cowboys. "That is the smartest hoss that ever walked God's earth! Why did you get rid of the poor bugger?"

"Why? You should not even ask why!" says the cowboy. "Whoever heard of a real cowboy using cream and sugar in his coffee!"

Drinking Horse

A man in Western attire walks into a Calgary bar and asks for 30 martinis in a big bucket.

"What?" says the bartender. "Why would you want so many martinis?"

"My horse likes 'em," replies the cowboy, "and he's tied to a parking meter out front dyin' of thirst. I want to surprise him."

So the bartender gets busy and makes a bucket of martinis.

"If you don't mind," says the bartender, "I'd like to see this boozing horse with my own eyes."

"Be my guest," says the customer, and the two men go outside and place the bucket by the horse, which begins to drink deeply.

"Darnedest thing I ever saw!" exclaims the bartender. "Why don't you come back inside the bar and I'll mix you a few martinis, on the house."

"No, I couldn't do that," says the man. "But thanks anyway."

"What's the matter?" asks the bartender. "Don't you like martinis?"

"Love 'em," replies the cowboy, "but I gotta drive."

Hi-ho, Silver, Away!

The Lone Ranger and his trusty sidekick Tonto are sitting and drinking in a bar when a cowboy comes in and asks, "Whose white horse is that outside?"

The Lone Ranger replies, "That's my horse, Silver."

"Well," says the cowboy, "he doesn't look too good. Seems the midday sun has got to him."

> **Cowboy Wisdom**
> Lettin' the cat outta the bag is a whole lot easier than puttin' it back.

The Lone Ranger and Tonto go outside and find Silver suffering in the heat. The Lone Ranger gives him a bowl of water and splashes some water across the horse's hide. The problem is that there is no breeze, so the Lone Ranger asks Tonto to run around Silver to get some air flowing to cool off the horse. So while Tonto is doing this, the Lone Ranger goes back into the bar to finish his drink.

Q: Why did the cowboy's car stop?

A: It had Injun trouble.

A few moments later, another cowboy walks into the bar and says, "Whose white horse is that outside?"

"What wrong with him now?" says the Lone Ranger.

"Nothing," replies the cowboy. "I just wanted to let you know that you left your Injun running."

Chapped Lips

Hell Peak is a town on the edge of a desert. It is the first stop for many travelers and cowboys after crossing through days of parched, lifeless landscape.

One day, a cowboy rides into town. He has been out in the sun for days. He gets off his horse, lifts its tail and kisses it where the sun don't shine.

"What you do that for?" asks a very shocked old-timer.

"Got chapped lips," replies the cowboy.

"And does that help?" asks the old man.

"Nope, it doesn't really help, but it does keep me from lickin' my lips."

Awwww

The doors to a saloon swing open and in limps a dog with one of his paws bandaged up. The normal din of the saloon dies away as every eye turns toward the dog.

The dog scans the bar, and then in a loud, clear voice says, "I'm lookin' fer the man who shot my paw!"

Measure Up

A bar has a sign in the window stating that anyone who can make the bartender's horse laugh will receive all the free drinks they want. A cowboy walks in and asks the bartender if he can give it a try, and the bartender tells him to go ahead.

The cowboy walks outside and whispers something in the horse's ear. The horse starts to laugh hysterically. The cowboy goes back into the bar, and the bartender gives him his free drinks.

The following night, the same cowboy walks into the bar, and the same thing happens. He whispers into the horse's ear, the horse laughs and the cowboy gets his free drinks.

On the third night, the sign is changed; this time, the offer is to make the horse cry. The same cowboy goes outside, and when he returns to the bar a few minutes later, the horse is crying.

The bartender says, "Okay, mister, you can have your free drinks, but first, tell me what you did to make my horse laugh."

"All I did was tell him that my dick is bigger than his," the cowboy explains.

"Okay, but how did you make him cry?" asks the bartender.

"I showed him!" replies the cowboy proudly.

Horse Sense

- I whisper to my horse, but he never listens.
- Grooming: the process by which the dirt on the horse is transferred to the groom.
- A woman needs two animals: the horse of her dreams and a jackass to pay for it.
- You never get the pleasure of owning a horse; you only have the pleasure of being its slave.
- May the Horse be with you!
- A horse ain't trying to be polite when he comes to a fence and allows you to go over first.
- A stubborn horse walks behind you, an impatient horse walks in front of you, but a noble companion walks beside you.
- There are only two emotions that belong in the saddle; one is a sense of humor and the other is patience.

Doh!

Two rattlesnakes are talking.

One of them turns to the other and asks, "Are we venomous?"

The other snake replies, "Yes, why do you ask?"

"I just bit me lip."

At the Water Cooler

Two horses are standing around talking near a water trough. One says to the other, "The boss has been riding me all day."

Wishful Thinking

It is early spring in the Old West. A cowboy riding the snow-choked trails is looking for cattle that survived the winter. As the cowboy's horse goes around the narrow trail, he comes upon a rattlesnake warming itself in the spring sunshine. The horse rears up, and the cowboy draws his six-gun to shoot the snake.

"Hold on there, partner," says the snake. "Don't shoot. I'm an enchanted rattlesnake, and if you don't shoot me, I'll grant you three wishes."

The cowboy decides to take a chance because he knows he is safely out of the snake's striking range. The cowboy says, "Okay. First, I'd like to have a face like Clark Gable; second, I want a body like Arnold Schwarzenegger; and finally, I'd like the same sexual equipment this here horse I'm riding has."

The rattlesnake says, "Alright. When you get back to your bunkhouse, you'll have all your three wishes."

The cowboy turns his horse around and gallops at full speed all the way to the bunkhouse. He dismounts on the run and goes straight inside the bunkhouse to the mirror. Staring back at him in the mirror is the face of Clark Gable. He rips the shirt off his back and sees bulging, rippling muscles, just like Arnold Schwarzenegger. Really excited now, the cowboy pulls down his jeans, looks at his crotch and shouts, "My God, I was riding the mare!"

Graffiti

A cowboy walks out of a saloon and finds that someone has painted his horse with whitewash. He storms back inside the bar and shouts, "Which one of you bastards whitewashed my horse?"

A huge gunslinger stands up and says, "Me. Why d'you want to know?"

"No reason," replies the cowboy. "Just thought I'd tell you that the first coat is dry."

Good Shooting

An old cowboy says to his grandson, "Sit here with your old man while I tell you a story. If there's anything I like to do more than telling stories, it's hunting. One day last week, I take my gun and go out to practice. I hit the bull's eye the first time, but it cost me $20 to pay for the bull.

> **Cowboy Wisdom**
> *If you're ridin' ahead of the herd, take a look back every now and then to make sure it's still there with ya.*

"But that is nothing compared to what happened to me last year. I'd been walking all day without seeing a thing to shoot at. I sits down on the bank of the river to rest. Pretty soon, I hear a noise upriver, and I see about 50 ducks. I cock my gun and take aim. Just as I am about to pull the trigger, I hear a noise down-river. I turn to look, and 100 geese are settling in. So I thinks to myself, 'I'd rather have geese than ducks,' so I aim at the geese.

"I'm about to squeeze off a shot when I hear a noise below me. I look down, and not three feet away I see a great big rattlesnake. Must be six-feet long if it's an inch, and it's coiled to strike, its mouth wide open. Well, son, I cock both barrels, take aim at the snake, squeeze the trigger and let go with both barrels. The dang gun bursts apart. The right-hand barrel flies upriver and kills the 50 ducks. The left-hand barrel shoots downriver and kills the 100 geese. The ram-rod shoots down the rattlesnake's throat and chokes it to death. The gunstock flies back and knocks me off my feet into the river, and I come out with my boots full of fish. Truer words, grandson, have never been spoken."

Q: What did the cowboy say when his dog fell in the fire?

A: Hot dog!

The Ventriloquist Cowboy

A ventriloquist cowboy walks into town and sees a rancher sitting on his porch with his dog at this feet.

Cowboy: "Hey, cool dog. Mind if I speak to him?"

Rancher: "This dog don't talk!"

Cowboy: "Hey, dog, how's it going?"

Dog: "Doin' alright."

The rancher has an extreme look of shock on his face.

Cowboy: "Is this your owner?" (pointing at the rancher)

Dog: "Yep."

Cowboy: "How does he treat you?"

Dog: "Real good. He walks me twice a day, feeds me great food and takes me to the lake once a week to play."

The rancher looks at the cowboy in disbelief.

Cowboy: "Mind if I talk to your horse?"

Rancher: "Horses don't talk!"

Cowboy: "Hey, horse, how's it goin'?"

Horse: "Cool."

The rancher is awestruck.

Cowboy: "Is this your owner?" (pointing at the rancher)

Horse: "Yep."

Cowboy: "How does he treat you?"

Horse: "Pretty good, thanks for asking. He rides me regularly, brushes me down often and keeps me in the barn to protect me from the elements."

The rancher is totally amazed.

Cowboy: "Mind if I talk to your sheep?"

Rancher (stuttering and hardly able to talk): "Th-Th-Them sheep ain't nothin' but liars!"

Know My Pet Monkey?

A mean cowboy has a pet monkey. One day as the two are walking down the street, the monkey jumps into the open window of a saloon. The cowboy goes after the monkey, and with his gun drawn, asks the people in the bar about his pet monkey.

"Do you know where is my pet monkey?" the cowboy asks the saloon owner.

"No," says the owner.

The cowboy shoots him dead.

He then asks a prostitute, "Do you know where is my pet monkey?"

"No," says the prostitute.

The cowboy shoots her too.

He then walks up to the piano player and says, "Do you know where is my pet monkey?"

"Yes, I know," says the pianist as he turns to his piano and begins to sing, "Where is my pet monkey, I wonder, taram, taram, pam-pam."

Divine Intervention

A devout cowboy loses his favorite Bible while he is mending fences out on the range.

Three weeks later, a cow walks up to him carrying the Bible in its mouth. The cowboy can't believe his eyes.

He takes the precious book out of the cow's mouth, raises his eyes heavenward and exclaims, "It's a miracle!"

"Not really," says the cow. "Your name is written inside the cover."

Cowboy Wisdom
Don't mess with somethin' that ain't bothering you.

At the Saloon

A horse walks up to the bar and orders a drink from the bartender. The bartender sets the drink in front of him and says to the horse, "It's okay, buddy, you can talk to me. Why the long face?"

Cowboy Pun

"I went riding today," says one cowboy to another.

"Horseback?" asks his friend.

"Yup!" replies the cowboy. "It came back before I did."

How Much for the Vet?

A cowboy takes his horse to the vet for a check-up.

The vet says to his assistant, "This horse is to pay only one-quarter of his bill."

The assistant asks why.

The vet replies, "Because he's a quarter horse!"

Flies

Visitor: "Wow, you have a lot of flies buzzing round your horses and cows. Do you ever shoo them?"

Cowboy: "No, we just let them go barefoot."

Good Reading

Bill: "Have you read the book, *100-mile Horse Trek*?"

Sam: "Who wrote it?"

Bill: "Major Bumsore."

What to Name Your Hoss

- Arrow
- Chompy
- Clint Eastwood
- Dead Eye
- Diamond Eye
- Lady Gaga
- Lightnin'
- Old Faithful
- Old Yeller
- Peanuts
- Red Hell
- SJP (Sarah Jessica Parker)
- Slick Willy
- Snake Eyes
- Straight Eye
- Sugar Dip
- Sylvester Stallion
- Whiskey Pete
- Willie Nelson

Buy a Horse

A guy calls his buddy, a horse rancher, and says he's sending over a friend who is looking to buy a horse.

His buddy asks, "How will I recognize your friend?"

"That's easy; he's a little person with a speech impediment."

The dwarf shows up at the rancher's home one day, and the rancher asks him if he's looking for a male or female horse.

"A female horth."

So the horse rancher shows him a prized filly.

"Nith lookin' horth. Can I thee her eyeth?"

The rancher picks up the dwarf, who gives the horse's eyes the once over.

"Nith eyeth, can I thee her earzth?"

The rancher picks the little fella up again and shows him the horse's ears.

"Nith earzth, can I thee her mouf?"

The rancher is getting pretty ticked off by this point, but he picks up the little man again and shows him the horse's mouth.

"Nice mouf, can I see her twat?"

Totally angry at this point, the rancher grabs the little man under his arms and rams the dwarf's head up the horse's fanny, pulls him out and slams him on the ground.

The midget gets up, sputtering and coughing.

"Perhapth I should rephrase that. Can I thee her wun awound a widdlebit?"

Gone Huntin'!

Two cowboys are out hunting. One of the cowboys has hunted all his life. The other has never hunted before.

The experienced hunter tells his friend to sit and be quiet in a tree stand while he scouts around. Then all of a sudden, the old hunter hears a blood-curdling scream. He runs over to his friend and says, "I thought I told you to be quiet."

Cowboy Wisdom
If you climb in the saddle, be ready for the ride.

The cowboy replies, "I didn't make a noise when the snakes slithered across my legs. I didn't make a sound when the bear breathed down my neck. But when those squirrels ran up my pants and I heard them say, 'Should we eat them now or take them with us?' I screamed."

Dead Donkey

Jean Paul moves to Kansas and buys a donkey for $100 from an old cowboy named Ben. The cowboy agrees to deliver the donkey the next day.

The next morning, Ben drives up to Jean Paul's ranch and says, "Sorry, but I have some bad news. The donkey died."

"Well, then, just give me the money back," says Jean Paul.

"Can't do that. I went and spent it already," replies Ben.

"Okay, then. Just unload the donkey and I'll take it," says Jean Paul.

"What ya going to do with him?" asks Ben.

"I'm going to raffle him off," says Jean Paul.

"You can't raffle off a dead donkey!" replies Ben.

"Sure can. Watch me. I just won't tell anyone that it's dead," says Jean Paul.

A month later, Ben meets up with Jean Paul and asks, "What happened with that dead donkey?"

"I raffled it off, I did. I sold 500 tickets at $2 apiece and made a profit of $898," says Jean Paul.

"Didn't anyone complain?" asks Ben.

"Just the guy who won. So I gave him his $2 back," says Jean Paul.

My Horse

My horse is brown, his teeth are white,
he has a long tail, he's quite a sight.
He eats grass all day, he lets out a neigh
to say he's okay.
I curry him down to make him bright,
he lets out a toot and I die of fright!

Long Ears

A cowboy owns a mule that is really docile until it has to be put into the stable. For some reason, when the mule is being loaded into the stable, its ears brush against the top of the doorway and the sensation makes it go crazy.

The cowboy decides to solve the problem by sawing away the upper part of the doorway, allowing the mule greater clearance. For hours the cowboy toils in the midday sun, hacking away at the wood. A passing neighbor points out to the cowboy that it would be a lot easier if he took a shovel and simply dug a shallow trench at the entrance.

Q: What has four legs and flies?

A: A dead horse.

The cowboy thanks the neighbor for the idea, but thinks to himself, "Stupid idiot! Anyone can see that it's not the mule's legs that are long, it's his ears!"

Making Headlines

A visitor to a small town in Texas is walking along the main street when he sees a wild dog leap out and attack a small boy. Without hesitation, the man takes out his six-shooter and shoots the dog dead.

The incident is witnessed by a reporter from the local newspaper. The reporter tells the man that the headline in that week's paper will be, "Brave Local Man Saves Child by Killing Rabid Beast."

"But I'm not from this town," says the man.

"No problem," replies the reporter. "The headline will read, 'Texas Man Saves Child by Killing Dog.'"

"As a matter of fact, sir," says the man. "I'm not from Texas at all. I'm from New York."

The reporter stares at the man and says, "In that case, the headline will read, 'Yankee Bastard Kills Family Pet.'"

Motivation

A woman offers the driver of a horse-drawn cab a large tip if he can deliver her to her destination in a hurry. However, she is horrified at the cruel whipping the driver is giving the horse to make it go faster.

"My good man, is there no other way you could urge the horse along?" she asks.

"Yessum," the cab driver cheerfully replies, "but I've got to save his balls for the hill!"

In the Theater

An old cowboy goes to town to see a movie. When he gets to the theater, the ticket girl says to him, "Sir, what is that on your shoulder?"

The cowboy says, "That is my pet rooster, Chuckie. Wherever I go, Chuckie goes."

"I'm sorry, sir," says the girl, "we don't allow animals in the theater. Not even a pet rooster."

The cowboy goes around the corner and stuffs the rooster down his pants. He returns to the booth, buys a ticket and enters the theater. He sits down next to two old nurses named Mildred and Marge.

The movie begins to play, and the rooster starts to squirm. The old cowboy unzips his jeans so Chuckie can stick his head out and watch the movie.

"Marge," whispers Mildred.

"What?" says Marge.

"I think the guy next to me is a pervert."

"What makes you think so?" asks Marge.

"He unzipped his pants, and he has his thing out," says Mildred.

"Well, don't worry about it," replies Marge. "At our age, it isn't anything we haven't seen before."

"Yes," says Mildred, "but this one is eating my popcorn!"

> **Cowboy Wisdom**
> Always drink upstream from the herd.

Flight Poetry

Birdie, birdie in the sky,
Dropped some white stuff in my eye.
I'm a big guy, I won't cry,
I'm just glad that cows don't fly.

Cock-a-doodle-doo

A rancher deep in the heart of Oklahoma buys a new rooster that turns out to be a total sex-crazed animal. It tears around the yard and mates with all the chickens, then when they are exhausted, the rooster goes for the ducks, the geese, then the turkeys. It is so horny that it even tries to jump a horse.

After the insatiable rooster has two weeks of frantic sex, the farmer is not surprised when he finds the bird lying flat on its back with a couple of buzzards circling overhead.

"I knew your heart would give out sooner or later, ya dumb bird!" says the rancher.

The rooster then opens one eye, looks at the buzzards, and whispers, "Get lost. You're gonna scare 'em away."

Know the Lingo

A city boy moves to Colorado wanting to start a ranch. He decides to start out small. He meets with a local farmer and says, "I want to buy a rooster, a chicken and a donkey."

"Sure," says the farmer, "but there's things you should know. 'Round here, we call a rooster, a *cock;* a chicken, a *pullet;* and a donkey, an *ass*. Now, I can sell you all three, but I must warn you, the ass is a mite ill-tempered, and if he tries to bite you, you have to scratch behind his ears to keep him calm."

So the city boy tucks the pullet and the cock under each arm and heads home riding the ass. As predicted, the ass tries to bite the man so he stops and gets off the ass. He recalls the advice of the farmer about scratching the animal's ears, but he can't do it because his hands are full. At that moment, a little old lady passes by.

Cowboy Wisdom
When in doubt, let your horse do the thinkin'.

"Excuse me," the man says. "Could you do me a favor? I need someone to hold my cock and pullet while I scratch my ass."

Vet Advice

Cowboy Jake goes to the vet and tells him that his horse is constipated. The vet hands him a bottle of pills and a tube and says, "Take one of these pills and put it in the tube, then stick the other end of the tube in your horse's anus. Then blow the pill up into its rectum."

Cowboy Jake leaves with the pills but returns the next day looking really ill.

"What happened?" asks the vet.

"It was the pill," replies the cowboy. "I did what you said, but the horse blew first."

How to Treat a Hero

A cowboy sees a farmer walking a pig and notices that the animal has one wooden leg. Curious, he asks the farmer how the pig lost its limb.

"Well," says the farmer, "one night the wife and me was asleep when the pig noticed from his pen that the house was on fire. He managed to break out of his pen, broke down our front door and dragged me to safety. Then it went back in the house and carried my wife out, then it rescued our four children. We'd all be dead if it weren't for this pig."

"So did the pig lose its leg in the fire then?" asks the cowboy.

"Oh no," says the farmer. "When you got a pig like this, you don't eat it all at once."

If a cow laughed, would milk come out its nose?

Reincarnation

A widow goes to visit a gypsy psychic who is able to contact the woman's deceased husband.

"Are you happy, dear?" the widow asks her husband.

"Yes," replies the husband. "I'm in a field surrounded by beautiful cows."

"Can you see any angels?" asks the wife.

"No, but there's a prize-winning cow standing in front of me. A real stunner," says her husband.

Thinking his answers are a little strange but normal for a cowboy, she asks, "Have you seen God?"

"No, but the cows are really, really fantastic."

"Why do you keep going on about cows? You lived your whole life surrounded by cows," asks the wife.

"Sorry," says the husband. "I forgot to mention—I'm back on our ranch. I've come back as a bull."

Mad Cows

Two cows are standing in a field. One says to the other, "Are you worried about mad cow disease?"

The other one says, "No, it doesn't worry me. I'm a horse!"

Car Trouble

An insurance salesman from the Calgary goes out to the farm community to sell insurance to the farmers. He is way out in the country when he has engine trouble. Not knowing anything about cars, he gets out and looks under the hood anyway.

All of a sudden, he hears a voice that says, "It's the carburetor."

The salesman jumps and looks around, but he doesn't see anyone. He then looks under the hood again, hoping it is something visible that he can fix himself, when he hears the voice again: "It's the carburetor."

The man jumps again, turns around and sees a large Brahma bull behind him. Scared out of his wits, he takes off running to the nearest farmhouse.

He knocks on the door, and when a farmer answers, the salesman immediately goes into his story about the bull.

The farmer scratches his head and says, "Does the bull have one straight ear and one floppy ear?"

The man nods and says, "Yes, Yes!"

The farmer laughs and says, "Don't worry about him. He doesn't know as much about cars as he thinks he does."

Q: If a cowboy rides into town on Friday and three days later leaves on Friday, how does he do it?

A: The horse's name is Friday!

Sink Hole

A horse and a chicken are playing in a meadow. The horse falls into a mud hole and is sinking. He tells the chicken to go and get the farmer to help pull him out to safety. The chicken runs to the farm, but the farmer can't be found. So the chicken drives the farmer's Mercedes back to the mud hole and ties some rope around the bumper. He then throws the other end of the rope to the horse and drives the car forward, saving his friend from sinking.

A few days later, the chicken and horse are playing in the meadow again, and the chicken falls into the mud hole. The chicken yells to the horse to go and get some help from the farmer. The horse says, "I think I can stand over the hole!" He spreads his back legs over the width of the hole and says, "Grab my thingy and pull yourself up." The chicken does as he is told and pulls himself to safety.

The moral of the story: if you're hung like a horse, you don't need a Mercedes to pick up chicks.

Good Trick

A cowboy walks into a bar and asks the bartender, "If I show you a really good trick, will you give me a free drink?" The bartender considers the offer then agrees. The man reaches into his pocket and pulls out a tiny rat. He reaches into his other pocket and pulls out a tiny piano. The rat stretches, cracks his knuckles and proceeds to play the blues on the piano.

After the man finishes his free drink, he asks the bartender, "If I show you an even better trick, will you give me free drinks for the rest of the evening?" The bartender agrees, thinking that no trick could possibly be better than the first.

The man reaches into his pocket and pulls out a small bullfrog, who begins to sing along with the rat's music.

Q: What is the difference between country music and cowboy music?

A: Country music is one guy singing about five women; cowboy music is five guys singing about one horse.

While the cowboy is enjoying his free drinks, a stranger confronts him and offers him $100,000 for the bullfrog.

"Sorry," the man replies, "he's not for sale."

The stranger increases the offer to $250,000, cash up front.

"No," he insists, "he's not for sale."

The stranger again increases the offer, this time to $500,000. The cowboy finally agrees, and hands over the frog to the stranger in exchange for the money.

"Are you insane?" says the bartender. "That frog could have been worth millions to you, and you let him go for a mere $500,000!"

"Don't worry about it," replies the cowboy. "The frog was really nothing special. You see, the rat is a ventriloquist."

Udder

A cowboy is milking one of his cows. He is just starting to get a good rhythm going when a bug flies into the barn and starts circling the cow's head. Suddenly, the bug flies into the cow's ear. The cowboy doesn't think much about it, until the bug squirted out into his bucket. It went in one ear and out the udder.

Pound for Pound

A man decides he wants to have a pig roast, so he goes out to a ranch to buy one. He agrees on a per-pound price with the farmer and then begins to select a pig. "How about that one?"

> **Cowboy Wisdom**
> Don't go in if you don't know the way out.

"Okay," replies the rancher. The rancher picks up the pig, puts its tail in his mouth and lets the pig hang from his mouth. He then declares, "This one weighs 74 pounds."

"That's amazing," the man says. "Are you sure you can tell a pig's weight by using that method?"

"Yep," says the rancher, "we've used this method in our family for generations." To prove his accuracy, the rancher puts the pig on a scale, and it weighs exactly 74 pounds.

"My son can do it, too," boasts the rancher. Sure enough, the rancher's son comes over, puts another pig's tail in his mouth, lets the pig hang down and then says, "This one weighs 83 pounds." The rancher confirms his son's accuracy with the scale.

"My wife can do it, too," says the rancher. "Son, go get your mother."

The boy runs off to the house and returns a few minutes later. "Mom can't come out right now," says the son. "She's busy weighing the mailman."

Bull Purchase

A middle-aged couple goes to an agricultural show way out in the countryside on a fine Sunday afternoon to watch the auctioning off of reproduction bulls. The guy selling the bulls announces the first bull to be auctioned off: "A fine specimen, this bull reproduced 60 times last year."

Cowboy Wisdom
Don't whine.

The wife nudges her husband in the ribs and comments, "See! That was more than five times a month!"

The second bull is to be sold: "Another fine specimen, this wonder reproduced 120 times last year."

Again the wife bugs her husband. "Hey, that's some 10 times a month. What do you say to that?"

Her husband is getting really annoyed with this comparison.

The third bull is up for sale: "And this extraordinary specimen reproduced 360 times last year!"

The wife slaps her husband on the arm and yells, "That's once a day, every day of the year! How about *you*?!"

The husband is pretty irritated by now and yells back, "Sure, once a day! But ask the announcer if they were all with the same cow!"

CHAPTER THREE

How Cowboys Do It

Oil Man

An Alberta oil baron goes to the dentist for a checkup. "I'm pleased to tell you that your teeth are fine," says the dentist.

"I know," replies the oilman, "but drill anyway. I'm feelin' lucky."

Three Brothers

A cowboy walks into a bar in Kansas City, orders three pints of beer and sits in the back of the room, taking a sip out of each pint in turn. When he finishes all three pints, he goes to the bar and orders three more.

So this cowboy walks into a German car dealership and says, "Audi!"

The bartender says to him, "You know, a pint goes flat after I draw it. The beer would taste better if you bought one at a time."

The cowboy replies, "Well, you see, I have two brothers. One is in Canada, and the other lives in New York City. When we all left home, we promised that we'd drink this way to remember the days when we drank together."

The bartender admits that this is a nice custom and leaves it at that. The cowboy becomes a regular in the bar and always drinks the same way: he orders three pints and drinks them in turn.

One day, he enters the bar and orders two pints. All the other regulars notice and fall silent. When he comes back to the bar for another round, the bartender says, "I don't want to intrude on your grief, but I would like to offer my condolences on your loss."

Q: How many ears did Davy Crockett have?

A: Three: the left ear the right ear and the wild front ear.

The cowboy looks confused for a moment then starts to laugh.

"Oh, no," he says. "Everyone's fine. I've just quit drinking."

Doc!

A man rushes into a doctor's office.

Man: "Doc! You gotta help me! I think I've got cowboy's disease!"

Doctor: "Hmmm. Tell me, how long have you had the symptoms?"

Man: "For about a yeee-harrr!"

The Mozart of Cowboys

A cowboy musician sees a "Piano Player Wanted" sign outside a bar. He goes in and explains that he's been playing for years. His repertoire includes old standards as well as many original tunes.

The manager asks him to play a few tunes, and the cowboy sits down and plays a beautiful piece of music.

"Wow, that was amazing! What do you call that song?" says the manager.

"I call it 'Horse Standing on my Crotch and Crushing my Balls,'" the cowboy says.

"Hmmm," says the manager, "play another song."

So the cowboy plays another even more beautiful song.

"That one is called, 'I Just Made Diarrhea in My Pants and My Dog Ate It,'" says the cowboy.

The manager decides to give the cowboy the job as long as he promises never to tell any of the customers the names of the songs. The cowboy agrees.

For weeks, things are going really well with the cowboy's new job, and the crowds love his music. One night after a great set, he takes a bathroom break and forgets to zip up.

> **Cowboy Wisdom**
> Tellin' a man to git lost and makin' him do it are two entirely different propositions.

A patron comes up to him a few minutes later and says, "Hey, do you know your pants are unzipped and your dick is hanging out?"

"Know it!" the cowboy says. "I wrote it!"

Gross! (I Warned You)

A stranger rides into a small Western town on a particularly hot, dry, dusty day. He gets off his swaybacked nag, dusts himself off and saunters into the nearest saloon.

"Gimme a whiskey," he drawls to the barkeep.

"Well, stranger," replies the wary proprietor, "I ain't seen you around here before and you look a little down on yer luck so I'd like to see some money on the bar before I start pourin' out my good likker."

"Ummm," says the stranger, "yer right. I don't have any money. How about just a sip of beer?"

"Costs a lot of money to bring beer here all the way from St. Louis, so I ain't about to give it away."

"Well, how about a glass of water then?" asks the newcomer.

"This place ain't got a really decent well, so water is about as scarce as beer and whiskey. Go find yerself another sucker, sucker."

"Look," retorts the stranger, "I got a powerful thirst, and I ain't a-leavin' here until I git somethin' to drink. I'll drink outta that spittoon if I hafta."

The bartender casts a glance at the nearly full spittoon on the floor near the end of the bar, and with a derisive snort, replies, "That'd be a new one. Nope, I don't believe anyone'd stoop that low."

Cowboy Wisdom
Don't squat with yer spurs on.

With that, the stranger grabs the cuspidor from the floor, wipes his mouth with the back of his hand, closes his eyes, tips the spittoon to his lips and commences a-gluggin'.

"I can't believe you'd actually do that," says the bartender with a grimace. He quickly pours out a large glass of water. "Here! Here's a glass of water. No charge!"

The stranger keeps on a-gluggin'.

The bartender quickly grabs another glass and fills it with beer. "Here! Best beer I got. On the house!"

The stranger keeps on a-gluggin'.

The bartender grabs a bottle of whiskey off the shelf and pours a shot. "I can't stand to watch this anymore. Here's your whiskey! Take the whole damn bottle!"

A few seconds later, the stranger sets the spittoon on the bar, grabs the shot glass of whiskey and pours it down, quickly followed by the entire beer and the entire glass of water.

"Why didn't you stop sooner?" asks the bartender. "That has to be the most disgusting thing I have ever witnessed!"

"Well," replies the stranger, "I caught onto a long one and I couldn't break it."

Cowboy Perspective

An Englishman has just returned home after visiting Texas and is telling his friends about his trip. One fellow asks, "What most impressed you about Texans?"

He replies, "Their confidence. A Texan took me out duck hunting, and we sat in a blind all day and never saw one duck. Then about sundown, a lone duck flies overhead, so high you could hardly see it. When it was directly overhead, the Texan raised his shotgun and fires. The duck keeps right on flying.

"The Texan turns to me in amazement and says, 'Son, yore witnessing a miracle. Thar flies a dead duck.'"

Strange Stranger

A Scot wanders into a cowboy bar. Two old cowboys are playing pool when they see this strangely dressed fellow. One of the cowboys points his pool cue toward the Scot's kilt.

"That shor is a cute little dressie," says the cowboy.

The Scot, offended, responds, "Would you be lookin' at me kilt?"

The cowboy replies, "Well, you shor will be kilt iffin you keep wearin' that little dressie 'round here."

Cowboy Computer Lingo Translation

Byte: Whut dem dang flies do.

Chip: Munchies fer watching the TV.

Click: Whut ya hear when ya cock yer gun.

Dot matrix: Ole Dan Matrix's wife.

Double click: When ya cock the double barrel.

Download: Gitten the firewood off'n the truck.

Enter: Northerner talk fer "C'mon in, y'all."

Floppy disk: Whut ya git from tryin' to tote too much firewood.

Hard drive: Gitten home in the wintertime.

Keyboard: Whar ya hang the dang truck keys.

Laptop: Whar the kitty sleeps.

Log off: Too much wood on fire.

Log on: Makin' a wood stove hot.

Main frame: Holds up the barn roof.

Megahertz: Whut ya git when ya git thrown off'n yer horse.

Micro chip: Whut's in the bottom of the munchie bag.

Modem: Whut ya do to the hayfields.

Monitor: Keep'n an eye on the wood stove.

Mouse pad: That's hippie talk fer where the mouse lives.

Mouse: Whut eats the grain in the barn.

Port: Fancy flatlander wine.

RAM: That thar thang whut splits the firewood.

Reboot: Whut ya have to do right before bedtime when ya have to go to the outhouse.

Screen: Whut to shut when it's black fly season.

Software: Dem dang plastic forks and knifes.

Windows: Whut to shut when it's cold outside.

The Quiet One

Three cowboys from Nebraska are sitting around a campfire, each possessing the bravado for which cowboys are famous. A night of tall tales begins.

The first cowboy says, "I must be the meanest, toughest cowboy there is. Why, just the other day, a bull got loose in the corral and gored six men before I wrestled it to the ground by the horns with my bare hands."

The second cowboy can't stand to be bested. "Why, that's nothing. I was walking down the trail yesterday, and a 15-foot rattlesnake slid out from under a rock and made a move for me. I grabbed that snake with my bare hands, bit its head off and sucked the poison down in one gulp. And I'm still here today."

The third cowboy remains silent, silently stirring the coals with his hands.

Fashion Priorities

A cowboy is galloping on the prairie. His inner voice says to him, "Turn left!" The cowboy immediately turns left, and an arrow flies to his right. The cowboy thinks, *My inner voice is good!* and he gallops forward more quickly.

The inner voice says to him again, "Turn right!"

The cowboy carries out the order immediately and another arrow flies to his left.

The cowboy thinks, *I will obey my inner voice always!*

The inner voice says to him again, "Take away the jeans!"

Q: What's the difference between a cowboy and a redneck?

A: The cowboy raises cattle; the redneck gets emotionally involved.

The cowboy does as he is told and a third arrow strikes the cowboy's ass.

"Why didn't you save me that time?" asks the cowboy to his inner voice. "It's painful!"

"But the jeans are safe!" says his inner voice.

> **Q:** Where do cowboys cook their meals?
>
> **A:** On the range.

Secret to a Long Life

A cowboy has lived to an extremely old age, and one day his grandson asks him to what he attributes his long life.

"Well, you know that every morning I have a bowl of oatmeal for breakfast," says the old-timer. His grandson nods. "Before I eat it, I sprinkle a little gunpowder on it, every day," the ancient cowpoke adds.

The grandson decides to follow his grandfather's breakfast regimen, and each morning for the rest of his life, he has oatmeal with gunpowder sprinkled on it.

Sure enough, the grandson lives to the ripe old age of 97, and when he dies, he leaves seven children, 21 grandchildren and 18 great-grandchildren—and a 15-foot hole in the side of the crematorium.

> **Cowboy Wisdom**
> Brace your backbone and forget your wishbone.

Where's the Party?

A drunk cowboy is brought before a judge.

The judge says, "You've been brought here for drinking."

The cowboy says, "Okay, let's get started."

Cowboy Medical Terms

Artery: The study of paintings.

Bacteria: Back door to cafeteria.

Barium: What doctors do when a cowboy dies.

Benign: What you be after you be eight.

Cat scan: Searching for Kitty.

Cauterize: Made eye contact with a pretty lady.

Cesarean section: A neighborhood in Rome.

Colic: A sheep dog.

Coma: A punctuation mark.

D&C: Where Washington is.

Dilate: To live long.

Enema: Not a friend.

Fester: Quicker than someone else.

Fibula: A small lie.

Genital: Non-Jewish person.

G.I. series: World Series of military baseball.

Hangnail: What you hang your coat on.

Impotent: Distinguished, well known.

Labor pain: Getting hurt at work.

Medical staff: A doctor's cane.

Morbid: A higher offer than I bid.

Nitrates: Cheaper than day rates.

Node: I knew it.

Outpatient: A person who has fainted.

Pap smear: A fatherhood test.

Pelvis: Second cousin to Elvis.

Post-operative: A letter carrier.

Recovery room: Place to do upholstery.

Rectum: Darn near killed him.

Secretion: Hiding something.

Seizure: Roman emperor.

Tablet: A small table.
Terminal illness: Getting sick at the airport.
Tumor: More than one.
Urine: Opposite of "you're out."
Varicose: Nearby.

Where Does it Hurt?

A midget cowboy down in Nevada complains to his buddy that his testicles ache almost all the time. As he is always complaining about this problem, his friend finally suggests that he go to a doctor to see what can be done to relieve the problem. The midget cowboy takes his advice and goes to the doctor and tells him about his problem.

The doctor tells him to drop his pants and he will have a look. The midget cowboy drops his pants, and the doctor puts him up on the examining table. The doc puts one finger under the little man's left testicle and tells him to turn his head and cough— the usual method to check for a hernia.

Q: Why did the bow-legged cowboy get fired?

A: Because he couldn't keep his calves together!

"Aha!" says the doc, putting his finger under the right testicle. He asks the midget to cough again. "Aha!" says the doctor as he reaches for his surgical scissors. Snip, snip, snip, snip on the right side, then snip, snip, snip, snip on the left side.

The midget is afraid to look, but he notes with amazement that the snipping did not hurt. The doctor then tells the midget to get dressed and see if his testicles still ache.

The midget cowboy is absolutely delighted as he walks around the doc's office and discovers his testicles no longer ache. "Gee, what did you do, Doc?" he asks.

The doc replies, "I cut two inches off the tops of your cowboy boots."

Gunslinging Lessons

In the days of the Wild West, there is a young cowboy who wants more than anything to be the greatest gunfighter in the world. He practices every minute of his spare time, but he knows that he isn't yet first-rate and that there must be something he is doing wrong.

Sitting in a saloon one Saturday night, he recognizes an elderly man sitting at the bar who has the reputation of being the fastest gun in the West.

The young cowboy takes the seat next to the old-timer, buys him a drink and tells him the story of his great ambition. "Do you think you could give me some tips?" he asks.

The old man looks the cowboy up and down and says, "Well, for one thing, you're wearing your gun too high. Tie the holster a lil' lower down on your leg."

"Will that make me a better gunfighter?" asks the young man.

"Sure will," says the old-timer.

The young man does as he is told, stands up, whips out his .44 and shoots the bow tie off the piano player.

"That's terrific!" says the cowboy, "Got any more tips for me?"

"Yep," says the old man. "Cut a notch out of your holster where the hammer hits it. That'll give you a smoother draw."

"Will that make me a better gunfighter?" asks the younger man.

"You bet it will," says the old-timer.

The young man takes out his knife, cuts the notch, stands up, draws his gun in a blur then shoots a cuff-link off the piano player.

"Wow!" says the cowboy. "I'm learnin' somethin' here. Got any more tips?"

The old man points to a large can in a corner of the saloon. "See that axle grease over there? Coat your gun with it."

Q: Why did the cowgirl plant bullets in her garden?

A: She wanted to grow bangs!

The young man goes over to the can and smears some of the grease on the barrel of his gun.

"No," says the old-timer, "I mean smear it all over the gun, handle and all."

"Will that make me a better gunfighter?" asks the young man.

"Nope," says the old-timer. "But when Wyatt Earp gets done playin' the piano, he's gonna shove that gun right up your ass, and it won't hurt as much."

Interview with a Cowboy

A reporter interviewing an old rancher asks him the secret to his success.

The rancher replies, "I don't know, but somethin' spurred me on."

Cheap Rider

A cowboy in Utah is so cheap that he goes into a general store and insists on buying just one spur for his boots.

"But, sir, I can't sell just one," says the shopkeeper. "They're a pair. You will have to buy both."

"I will not, sir," replies the cowboy. "I have a smart horse so all I need is one spur because where one side of the horse goes, the other side always follows."

Cowboy Wisdom

When you give a lesson in meanness to a critter or a person, don't be surprised if they learn their lesson.

Lucky Day!

A cowboy is walking through the prairies when he comes across a lamp. He picks it up and rubs it, and a genie pops out. As is customary, the genie grants the cowboy three wishes.

"I'd like 10 million dollars!" says the cowboy. Poof! Ten million dollars appears before his feet.

"I'd like a 1000-acre ranch!" Poof! He reappears on a beautiful ranch.

"I'd like to be irresistible to women!" Poof! He turns into a box of chocolates.

Cowboy Slang and Sayin's

- That boy ain't right—his family tree must be a shrub.
- He doesn't have nuthin' under his hat but hair.
- That cowgirl is as hot as a widowed coyote.
- He is so lazy that molasses wouldn't run down his legs.
- He's about as worthless as a pail of hot spit.
- That gal has no trouble gettin' a rake to gather her crop.
- She strayed off the main trail before her soul was full-growed.
- The water is deep 'nough to wash a high hoss' wither region.
- He's so tough that he chews up nails an' spits out tacks.
- That Billy is so tough that he grew horns.
- He is tougher than the calluses on a barfly's elbow.
- He is so weak that he couldn't lick his upper lip.
- John is wilder than a turpentined cat and as smart as a tree full of owls.
- That boy is so dumb that he can't drive a nail in a snowbank or tell a skunk from a housecat.

Piss

A drunk cowboy in a saloon finishes his beer and slams the glass on the bar.

"Piss!" he yells then asks for another. He downs that one too and again slams the empty glass down saying, "Piss!"

This happens again and again until the bartender looks the drunk in the face and says, "Piss off!"

The cowboy replies, "Oh, in that case, I'll have a whiskey."

Not a Cowboy Drink

A cowboy walks into a bar and orders a martini. The bartender brings his drink, and the cowboy fishes the olive out and puts it in a jar. He orders another and does exactly the same thing. The cowboy repeats this until he has a pile of olives in his jar on the bar.

"Excuse me," says the bartender, "but is something wrong with the drink?"

"Oh, no," replies the cowboy. "The wife sent me out to get a jar of olives."

Just Try Me!

Cowboys are always trying to outdo one another. Two cowboys are sitting around drinking. One cowboy says to the other, "I bet I could gross you out."

The other guy says, "No way you could gross me out. Whatever you do, I can top it."

So the first guy vomits all over the table.

The second cowboy looks at him, laughs and pulls out a straw.

Cowboy Olympics

A Russian and a Kansas cowboy wrestler are set to square off for the Olympic gold medal. Before the final match, the cowboy wrestler's trainer walks up to him and says, "Now, don't

Q: What office did the female horse run for?

A: Mare.

forget all the research we've done on this Russian. He's never lost a match because of this 'pretzel' hold he has. Whatever you do, don't let him get you in that hold! If he does, you're finished!"

The cowboy nods in acknowledgment. As the match starts, the cowboy and the Russian circle each other several times, looking for an opening.

All of a sudden, the Russian lunges forward, grabbing the cowboy and wrapping him up in the dreaded pretzel hold. A sigh of disappointment rises from the crowd, and the trainer buries his face in his hands because he knows all is lost. He can't watch the inevitable happen.

Suddenly, there is a scream, then a cheer from the crowd, and the Kansas trainer raises his eyes just in time to see the Russian go flying up in the air. The Russian's back hits the mat with a thud, and the cowboy wrestler collapses on top of him, making the pin and winning the match.

Cowboy Wisdom
Always keep your head up, unless you're walking in a cow pasture.

The trainer is astounded. When he finally gets his wrestler alone, he asks, "How did you ever get out of that hold? No one has ever done it before!"

The wrestler replies, "Well, I was ready to give up when he got me in that hold, but at the last moment, I opened my eyes and saw a pair of testicles right in front of my face. I had nothing to lose, so with my last ounce of strength, I stretched out my neck and bit those babies just as hard as I could."

"So," the trainer exclaims, "that's what finished him off!"

"Not really," says the cowboy wrestler. "You'd be amazed how strong you get when you bite your own nuts."

Cowgirl

This big, nasty, sweaty cowgirl wearing a sleeveless sundress walks into a bar. She raises her right arm, revealing a big, hairy armpit as she points to all the people sitting at the bar and asks, "What man out there will buy a lady a drink?" The whole bar goes dead silent, as the patrons try to ignore her.

Q: Why was the pig wearing cowboy boots?

A: Because he was going to a country swine dance.

At the end of the bar, a skinny little drunk cowboy slams his hand on the bar and says, "Bartender! I want to buy that ballerina a drink!" The bartender pours the drink, and the woman chugs it down.

After she downs the drink, she turns to the patrons and points around at all of them, again revealing her hairy armpit, saying, "What man out there will buy a lady a drink?"

Once again, the little drunk slaps his hand down on the bar and says, "Bartender! I'd like to buy the ballerina another drink!"

After serving the woman her drink, the bartender approaches the little drunk and says, "It's your business if you want to buy the lady a drink, but why do you call her a ballerina?"

The cowboy replies, "Sir! In my eyes, any woman who can lift her leg up that high has got to be a ballerina!"

Davy

One fateful day, Davy Crockett wakes up and walks from his bunk on the floor of the Alamo up to the observation post on the west wall.

William B. Travis and Jim Bowie are up there already. The three men gaze at the hordes of Mexicans moving steadily toward them.

Davy turns to Bowie with a puzzled look on his face and says, "Jim, are we landscaping today?"

Cowboy Wisdom

Any cowboy can carry a tune. The trouble comes when he tries to unload it.

Bar Talk

A cowboy walks into a saloon. The bartender says, "You've got a steering wheel down your pants."

"Yeah, I know," says the cowboy. "It's driving me nuts."

Nicknames for the Camp Cook

- Dough Boy
- Grease Belly
- Grub Worm
- Meat Master
- The Jolly Fryer
- Montezuma's Revenge
- Mother Hen (But don't dare say that to his face.)
- Old Lady (I wouldn't call him that one either.)

On a Plane

An Oklahoma cowgirl and a girl from the East Coast are seated side by side on an airplane.

The cowgirl, being friendly and all, says, "So, where y'all from?"

The East Coast girl says, "From a place where they know better than to use a preposition at the end of a sentence."

The cowgirl sits quietly for a few moments and then replies with a sweet smile and her fabulous sticky-sweet drawl, "So, where y'all from, *bitch*?"

> **Cowboy Wisdom**
> The man who wears his holster tied down don't do much talkin' with his mouth.

CHAPTER FOUR

Out to Pasture

Rain

A cowboy from the north rides into Texas for the first time and asks a rancher, "Does it ever rain here?"

The rancher replies, "Yes. Remember that part in the Bible where it rained for 40 days and 40 nights?"

"Of course, you mean Noah's flood?"

"Yep, well, we got about two inches durin' that spell, I reckon."

Varmint

A cowboy walks into the office of an insurance company in Vancouver and tries to buy health insurance. The insurance agent is going down the list of standard questions when he asks, "Have you ever had an accident?"

"Nope," says the cowboy. "Ain't never had none."

"Never?" the agent says. "Well, you wrote on this form that you were bit by a snake once. Wouldn't you consider that an accident?"

Cowboy Wisdom
Don't worry about bitin' off more'n you can chew; your mouth is probably a whole lot bigger'n you think.

"Heck, no!" replies the cowboy. "That dang varmint bit me on purpose."

Bear Hunting?

Cowboy John goes bear hunting and spots a small brown bear and shoots it. Suddenly, he feels a tap on his shoulder, and he turns around to see a big black bear.

The black bear says, "You've got two choices. I either maul you to death, or we have sex."

John decides to bend over.

Even though he feels sore for two weeks, John soon recovers and vows revenge. He heads out on another trip, where he finds the black bear and shoots it.

There is another tap on John's shoulder. This time, a huge grizzly bear stands right next to John.

The bear says, "That was a huge mistake, John. You've got two choices. Either I maul you to death, or we'll have rough sex." Again, John thinks it is better to bend over.

> **Q:** Why did the cowboy keep his horse in a barn?
>
> **A:** To give it a stable environment.

John survives, but it takes several months before he fully recovers. Outraged, he heads back to the woods, tracks down the grizzly and shoots it. He feels sweet revenge, but then he feels a tap on his shoulder. He turns around to find a giant polar bear standing there.

The polar bear says, "Admit it, John. You don't come here for the hunting, do you?"

Lonely West

A lawyer from New York is transferred to a small frontier town in Kansas during the settlement of the West. After several weeks there, he notices that the place is populated solely by men.

He asks one of the local cowboys, "What do you do when you get the urge for a woman?"

The cowboy replies, "See them thar sheep up on that hill? We just go git us one."

"That is disgusting and barbaric!" replies the lawyer.

Q: Who is the fittest and leanest cowboy in the West?

A: The Toned Ranger.

But after about three months, the lawyer can't stand the loneliness any longer. He decides, though, that if he is going to do a sheep, he will show these yokels how to do it right. Picking out the prettiest sheep of the flock, the lawyer bathes and sprinkles perfume on her and puts a pink ribbon around her neck. Then he serves her hay on a china plate, dresses her in fine lingerie and then takes the sheep to bed.

After finishing, the lawyer decides to take his new-found "lover" out for a drink. He wanders into the local saloon with the sheep under his arm. The piano falls silent, people drop their drinks and all the cowboys turn and stare in shocked disbelief.

The lawyer shouts, "You bunch of hypocrites! You look at me as if I'm some sort of freak for doing what you've been doing all along! I'm just going about it with more class!"

"That ain't the problem," one cowboy replies. "The problem is…that's the sheriff's gal you got with ya."

More Sheep

A cowboy from Montana and a cowboy from California are on a sheep drive. They have been out for weeks and have been pulling sheep out of the mud and working really hard. Eventually they come across a sheep with her head stuck in the fence.

They are both very lonely, so the cowboy from Montana says, "I'm first!" and he drops his pants and mounts the sheep. When he is finished, he steps back, looks at the California cowboy and says, "You're next."

The California cowboy drops his pants and sticks his head in the fence.

Life on the Range

I remember Dad telling me that the winter of 1929 was the coldest winter he remembered. At the time, he was living by himself on his uncle's ranch, helping out with the chores and seeing to the animals. As there was no electricity, he used a kerosene lamp for light, and on really cold nights, he used the lamp to get a bit of heat.

> **Cowboy Wisdom**
> Never approach a bull from the front, a horse from the rear or a fool from any direction.

My dad told me that one night it got so cold that the flame literally froze in the lamp. It stayed frozen for three days and nights. On the morning of the fourth day, my dad got tired of looking at that sad little frozen flame that was giving off no heat, so he broke it off and threw it out the window into the yard.

My dad's uncle always kept some chickens in the yard. After the ground was frozen-over for a week or so, the chickens were ready to eat anything that moved.

When one of the chickens saw that flame sliding across the ice, she ran over, plucked it up and swallowed it. That chicken laid hard-boiled eggs for a week after that.

Cowpoke

More than anything, Bobby wants to be a cowpoke. Taking pity on him, a rancher hires the lad and gives him a chance.

"This," he says, showing the boy a rope, "is a lariat. We use it to catch cows."

"I see," says Bobby, trying to seem knowledgeable as he examines the lariat. "And what do you use for bait?"

Them City Folks Again!

A rancher is watching a city slicker trying to saddle a horse for the first time. In an effort to be helpful, the rancher says, "Pardon me, sir, but yer puttin' the saddle on the wrong way."

The city slicker angrily snaps back, "Mind your own damn business! You don't even know which direction I'm going!"

Q: Did you hear about the fugitive baker cowboy?

A: He was Wanted Bread or Alive.

Ode to Arizona

The Devil wanted a place on earth.
Sort of a summer home:
A place to spend his vacation
Whenever he wanted to roam.

So he picked out Arizona.
A place both wretched and rough.
Here the climate was to his liking
And the cowboys were hardened and tough.

He dried up the streams in the canyons
And ordered no rain to fall:
He dried up the lakes in the valleys,
Then baked and scorched it all.

Then over his barren desert
He transplanted shrubs from Hell.
The cactus, thistle and prickly pear—
The climate suited them well.

Now, the home was much to his liking.
But animal life, he had none,
So he created crawling creatures
That all mankind would shun.

First he made the rattlesnake.
With its forked poisonous tongue,
Taught it to strike and rattle
And how to swallow its young.

Then he made scorpions and lizards
And the ugly old horned toad.
He placed spiders of every description
Under rocks by the side of the road.

Then he ordered the sun to shine hotter.
Hotter and hotter still.
Until even the cactus wilted
And the old horned toad looked ill.

Then he gazed on his earthly kingdom.
As any creator would.
He chuckled a little up his sleeve
And admitted that it was good.

'Twas summer now and Satan lay
By a prickly pear to rest.
The sweat rolled off his earthy brow.
So he took off his coat and vest.

"By Golly," he finally panted,
"I did my job too well.
I'm going back where I came from.
Arizona is hotter than Hell!"

(source: www.ahajokes.com)

Lost by the River

A dumb cowboy is lost near a river. He walks up and down it, searching for a way to get to the other side.

He tries walking in the shallow part of the river, and he even tries grabbing onto a branch that stretches halfway across the river in order to swing to the other side. No matter how hard he tries, though, he can't get across.

Q: Why can't the bankrupt cowboy complain?

A: He ain't got no beef.

After many failed attempts, he feels like giving up. But, at the last moment, he sees a man walking by and decides to follow him—across the bridge.

Bull Mate

A blonde and a brunette are running a ranch together in Wyoming. The two women decide they need a bull to mate with their cows to increase their herd. The brunette takes their lifesavings of $600 and goes to Colorado to buy a bull. She eventually meets with an old cowboy who is willing to sell her a bull.

"It's the only one I got for $599, take it or leave it."

She buys the bull and goes to the local telegram office and says to the clerk, "I'd like to send a message to my friend in Wyoming that says, 'Have found the stud bull for our ranch; bring the trailer.'"

The man behind the counter tells her, "Telegrams to anywhere in the U.S. are $0.75 per word."

She thinks about it for a moment and makes a decision. "I'd like to send one word, please."

"And what word would that be?" inquires the man.

"Comfortable," replies the brunette.

The man says, "I'm sorry, Miss, but are you sure your friend is gonna understand this telegram?"

The brunette replies, "My friend is blonde and reads *real* slow. When she gets this, she will see 'com-for-da-bull.'"

Out Shooting

A guy takes his greenhorn wife hunting near a ranch. When they reach their deer blinds, the husband says to his wife, "If you shoot a deer, be sure not to let somebody else say he's the one who shot it. Otherwise, he'll take the deer from you. The deer belongs to whoever shoots it."

> **Cowboy Wisdom**
> Don't dig for water
> under the outhouse.

The guy walks over to his own blind. Ten minutes later, he hears his wife shooting from her blind nearby. He rushes over and finds her pointing her rifle at a cowboy who's hollering, "Awright, lady, awright—you can have the goddamn deer! Just lemme get my saddle off it!"

Frontier Town

A pastor at a frontier church ends a stirring sermon with, "All those who want to go to heaven, put up your hands!"

Everybody enthusiastically raises their hands—everybody except a grizzled old cowboy who is slouching against the door post at the back of the church.

All heads turn as the cowboy saunters up to the front, spurs jangling, and says, "Preacher, that was too easy. How do you know if these folks are serious? I can guarantee I can prove who really means it and who don't!"

Bemused, the preacher says, "Okay, stranger, go ahead and put the faith of these good people to the test. Ask them anything you want."

At that, the cowboy pulls out his twin six-shooters, turns to the congregation and says, "All right...who wants to go heaven...raise your hands!"

Guide

Lone Ranger and Tonto are riding across the plains when Tonto stops suddenly, gets off his horse and puts his ear to the ground.

Lone Ranger waits a few minutes then asks Tonto, "What is it?"

"Buffalo come," Tonto replies.

"How can you tell?"

"Ear sticky."

Peaceful?

Tom has been in police work for 25 years. Finally sick of the stress, he quits his job and buys 50 acres of land in the middle of Montana as far from humanity as possible. He sees the postman once a week and gets groceries once a month. Otherwise, he is surrounded by total peace and quiet.

After six months or so of almost total isolation, someone knocks on his door. He opens it, and a huge bearded man is standing there.

"Name's Cliff, your neighbor from 40 miles up the road. Havin' a Christmas party Friday night. Thought ya might like to come at about five o'clock."

"Great," says Tom. "After six months out here by myself, I'm ready to meet some local folks. Thank you."

As Cliff is leaving, he stops, turns around and says, "Gotta warn you. Be some drinkin'."

"Not a problem," says Tom. "After 25 years in the business, I can drink with the best of 'em."

The big man starts to leave and stops again. "More'n likely gonna be some fightin' too."

"Well, I get along with people. I'll be all right. I'll be there. Thanks again!"

"More'n likely be some wild sex too."

"That's really not a problem," replies Tom, warming to the idea. "I've been all alone for six months! I'll definitely be there. By the way, what should I wear?"

"Don't much matter. Just gonna be the two of us."

Out in the Cold

On a cold winter day, two cowboys are traveling by horseback in Alberta. It is colder than a mother-in-law's kiss. One cowboy has on red flannel underwear, a woolen shirt, heavy pants, a jacket and an overcoat, while the other cowboy is wearing nothing but his underwear and a blanket. Despite all the clothing the one cowboy is wearing, the wind still cuts through like a knife while his friend shows no signs of the chill.

"Aren't you cold, pardner?" asks the dressed cowboy.

"Nope," says the half-naked cowboy.

"I don't understand it. Here I am wrapped up in all the clothes I have to my name and I'm about to freeze to death, and all you have on is that flimsy blanket and your drawers, and you says you ain't cold!"

"Is your face cold?" asks the half-naked cowboy.

"No, my face ain't cold!"

"Well, I'm all face."

Q: What's the nearest thing to silver?

A: The Lone Ranger's bum.

Gone Fishin'

Two cowboys in British Columbia go down to the local fishing hole on their day off. One cowboy gets a bite within the first two minutes and pulls out a 50-pound salmon. Not wanting to keep it, he is just about to throw it back into the water when the other cowboy screams, "Wait! Don't throw it away just yet."

"Why?"

"'Cuz we gots to brand it," says the cowboy, pulling out a red-hot cattle branding iron from the fire.

"Why in God's name would you want to brand a salmon?" asks his friend.

"Simple," replies the cowboy. "Just in case any other fisherman might try to claim it as part of his herd."

Lost

A man new to life in the West gets himself lost in open country. He spends several days wandering through forests, through flat grasslands and through dry valleys and still finds no signs of civilization. A few more days like this, and he would surely die. But God shows him some mercy when a cowboy comes slowly riding toward him.

> **Cowboy Wisdom**
> The biggest trouble-maker you'll ever deal with watches you shave his face every morning.

"Oh, thank the Lord I found you!" says the tenderfoot cowboy. "How far is it to town?

"'Bout a half a quart down the trail," replies the drunken cowhand.

A Cowboy Drunk Meter

Words that are difficult for a cowboy to say when he's drunk:
- Innovative
- Preliminary
- Proliferation
- Cinnamon

Terms that are *extremely* difficult for a cowboy to say when he's drunk:
- Specificity
- British constitution
- Passive-aggressive disorder
- Transubstantiate

Sentences that are *absolutely impossible* for a cowboy to say when he's drunk:
- Thanks, but I don't want to sleep with you.
- Nope, no more booze for me.
- Sorry, but yer not really my type.
- No kebab for me, thank you.
- Good evening, sheriff. Ain't it lovely out tonight?
- I ain't interested in fightin' you.
- Oh, I just couldn't—no one wants to hear me sing.
- Thank you, but I won't make any attempt to dance. I have no coordination. I'd hate to look like a fool.
- Where is the nearest toilet? I refuse to vomit in the street.
- I have to go home now because I gotta work in the mornin'.

Be Nice to the Cook

When out moving cattle, it always made the long days much easier to have a good cook along for the ride. Old Pete is the worst cook in all the prairies, and he is also one of the meanest SOBs in all the lands. Every time the dinner bell rings, the ranchers know Old Pete will be in a foul mood. But the ranchers put up with his temper and his bad food, so they just quietly stare down at their plates and eat. One time during dinner, a new cowhand is not enjoying his meal. Before anyone can stop the poor feller, he walks over to Old Pete and complains about his stew being cold and the meat tasting a bit off.

Old Pete starts to jump up and down with joy, pulling off his apron and kissing the new cowhand on the cheek. Old Pete then grabs a bottle of whiskey and disappears into his tent. Confused, the new cowhand looks around and asks what just happened.

"Well, you see," replies one of the older cowboys, "a long time ago, Old Pete was a young inexperienced cowhand like yourself. He knew nothing of the cowboy way of life, and one day, at dinner time, he decides to tell our old cook what he thought of his dinner, and that's how he became our cook."

"I don't understand," replies the young cowhand.

"Well, you see, we cowboys have few rules, but one of the most sacred is that if you complain about the cooking—you become the cook!"

Abandoned Shack

They say the open lands of the West are the healthiest lands on earth, given that no one has ever died naturally.

Note found on an abandoned shack left by an eastern city boy who came to seek his fortune in the middle of Nevada:

"30 miles to water.
20 miles to wood.
10 inches to Hell.
Gone back east to wife's family!"

Out Hunting

A cowboy takes his wife and his mother-in-law out hunting. One evening, as the cowboy and his wife are sitting by the campfire having supper, they suddenly realize that the mother-in-law is missing.

The cowboy picks up his rifle, and with his wife close behind, they set off into the forest to look for the missing woman.

After searching for over an hour, they finally spot her—she is backed up against a cliff with a huge bear facing her.

"What are we going to do?" screams the wife.

"Nothing," replies the cowboy. "The bear done got himself into this mess."

New to Town

A stranger walks into a rundown bar in the middle of nowhere in Utah and orders a pink martini. All the heads in the bar immediately turn and glare at the stranger.

The bartender says, "You ain't from round these parts, are ya?"

"No," says the stranger. "I'm from Maine."

"Yeah?" says the bartender. "What d'you do up in Maine?"

"Why, I am a taxidermist," replies the stranger.

"A taxidermist?" says the bartender. "What's a *tax-i-der-mist?*"

"It's someone who stuffs and mounts dead animals," explains the stranger.

Hearing this, the bartender yells out to the other customers, "It's okay, boys, he's one of us!"

Mr. Know-It-All

A rancher is sitting on his porch one day when a young man drives up to his home and walks up to the door. "Sir, I was driving by and noticed you had a lot of milkweed in your pasture. Would you mind if I went out and got some milk?"

Q: What kind of robbery is the easiest?

A: A safe robbery.

"You don't get milk from milkweed!" the rancher replies.

"Oh, yes, I know that," says the young man. "I have a degree in agriculture from Texas A&M."

"Well, help yourself," says the rancher. A few minutes later, the rancher sees the young man walking back to his car with two buckets full of milk.

The next day, the rancher is again sitting on his porch when the same young man drives up.

"Sir, yesterday when I was getting milk, I noticed you had some honeysuckle in the fence row. I wondered if you would mind if I got some honey?"

"You don't get honey from honeysuckle!" says the rancher. Again, the young man explains about his degree from A&M, so the rancher agrees to let him collect some honey.

The young man soon returns with two buckets full of honey and drives off.

The next day, the same young man drives up to the rancher's house again.

"Sir, yesterday when I was getting the honey, I noticed you had some pussy willows down by the creek."

The rancher says, "Let me get my boots, and I'll go with ya!"

City Boy

A young man from the city goes to visit his uncle who is a rancher. For the first few days, the uncle shows his nephew the usual things—cows, chickens, crops and so on. After three days, however, it is obvious that his nephew is getting bored, and the uncle is running out of things to amuse him with.

Cowboy Wisdom
When a cowboy is too old to set a bad example, he hands out good advice.

Finally, the uncle has an idea. "Why don't you grab a gun, take the dogs and go shooting?" This seems to cheer up the nephew, and with renewed enthusiasm, off he goes into the field, with the dogs running ahead of him.

After a few hours, the nephew returns.

"How did you enjoy that?" asks his uncle.

"It was great!" exclaims the nephew. "Got any more dogs?"

Estimated Value

A motorist driving by a Texas ranch hits and kills a calf crossing the road.

The driver finds the owner of the calf and explains what happened. He then asks the rancher what the animal was worth.

"Oh, about $200 today," says the rancher. "But in six years, it would have been worth $900. So $900 is what I'm out."

The motorist sits down and writes out a check and hands it to the rancher.

"Here," the man says. "It's a check for $900. It is post-dated six years from now."

Big Hole

A cowboy is walking through a field when he stumbles onto a hole. He throws a stone in the hole to see how deep it is. He doesn't hear anything, so when he spots a large boulder, he throws it into the hole.

As he is waiting for a sound, he sees a ram suddenly charging toward him. At the last moment, the cowboy jumps out of the way, and the ram plummets down the hole.

Later on that day, the cowboy meets the landowner and tells him that the hole in his field is very dangerous.

"I know," replies the landowner. "That's why I put a big ram in the field—to scare away the children."

"Really?" says the cowboy. "But what happens if the ram wanders off?"

"Oh, it can't do that," replies the man. "I tied it to a large boulder."

Duck Hunting

Two cowboys from Saskatchewan are on vacation and go duck hunting. One cowboy shoots at a flying bird and it falls dead at his feet.

"You could've saved yourself a shot there," says the other cowboy. "From that height, the fall alone would've killed it."

Smart Doggy

Cowboys Chester and Earl are deciding whether to go hunting. Chester says to Earl, "I'll send my dog out to see if any ducks are in the pond. If there aren't any ducks there, I'm not going hunting."

Chester sends the dog out to the pond. The dog comes back and barks twice. Chester says, "Well, I'm not going hunting. My dog only saw two ducks."

Earl says, "You're going to take the dog's barks for the truth?" Earl doesn't believe it, so he goes to the pond to look for himself. When he gets back, he says, "I don't believe it—where did you get that dog? There really are only two ducks out there!"

Chester says, "Well, I got him from the breeder up the road. If you want, you can get a dog from the breeder, too."

Earl goes to the breeder and says he wants a dog like the one his friend Chester has. The breeder obliges, and Earl takes the dog hunting with him and tells it to go out and look for ducks. Minutes later, the dog returns with a stick in its mouth and starts humping Earl's leg.

Outraged, Earl takes the dog back to the breeder and says, "This dog is a fraud! I want my money back!"

The breeder asks Earl what the dog did. Earl tells him that when he sent the dog out to look for ducks, it came back with a stick in its mouth and started humping his leg.

The breeder says, "Earl, all he was trying to tell you was that there are more ducks out there than you can shake a stick at!"

Poor Boy

A wandering cowboy from Calgary walks up to the front door of a neat-looking farmhouse in rural Alberta and raps gently on the door. When a farmer opens the door, the cowboy says, "Please, sir, could you give me something to eat? I haven't had a good meal in several days."

> **Q:** Who's the fastest cowboy in the Wild West?
>
> **A:** Sprint Eastwood.

The farmer says, "I have made a fortune in my lifetime by supplying goods for people. I've never given anything away for nothing. However, if you go around the back, you will see a gallon of paint and a clean paintbrush. If you paint my porch, I will give you a good meal."

The cowboy goes around back, and a few hours later, he again knocks on the farmer's door. The owner opens the door and says, "Finished already? Good! Come on in. Sit down. The cook will bring your meal right in."

The cowboy says, "Thank you very much, sir. But there's something that I think you should know. It's not a Porsche you got there. It's a BMW."

Cross the Road

A cowboy is driving his truck down a quiet country lane when out into the road strays a rooster. Whack! The rooster disappears under the truck. A cloud of feathers floats in the air.

Shaken, the cowboy pulls over at the nearest farm-house and rings the doorbell. A farmer opens the door. The cowboy, somewhat nervously, says, "Sorry, I think I killed your rooster. Please allow me to replace him."

"Suit yourself," the farmer replies. "You can go join the other chickens 'round back."

Pull!

An out-of-towner accidently drives his truck into a ditch in a desolate area in Saskatchewan. Luckily, a local farmer wanders by and offers to help get him out, with his big strong horse named Buddy. The farmer hitches Buddy up to the truck and yells, "Pull, Nellie, pull!" But Buddy doesn't move.

Then the farmer hollers, "Pull, Buster, pull!" Buddy doesn't respond.

Once more the farmer commands, "Pull, Coco, pull!" Nothing.

Finally, the farmer nonchalantly says, "Pull, Buddy, pull!" And the horse easily drags the truck out of the ditch.

The driver is most appreciative and is curious about what has just happened. He asks the farmer why he called his horse by the wrong name three times.

The farmer says, "Oh, Buddy is blind, and if he thought he was the only one pulling, he wouldn't even try!"

Lawyer

A big-city lawyer is representing a railroad in a lawsuit filed by an old rancher. The rancher's prize bull is miss-ing from the section through which the railroad passed.

The rancher claims that the bull was hit by the train, and he wants to be paid the fair value of the bull.

As soon as the rancher shows up in court, the attorney for the railroad pulls him aside and tries to get him to settle out of court. The lawyer does his best sell job, and finally the rancher agrees to take half of what he was asking.

Cowboy Wisdom
Never ask a barber if you need a haircut.

After the rancher signs the release and takes the check, the young lawyer can't resist gloating a little over his success, telling the rancher, "You know, I hate to tell you this, old man, but I put one over on you in there. I couldn't have won the case. The train engineer was asleep when the train went through your ranch that morning. I didn't have one witness to put on the witness stand. I bluffed you!"

The old rancher replies, "Well, I'll tell you, young feller, I was a mite worried about winnin' that case myself because that darned bull came home this mornin'."

At the Store

A cowboy farmer from back in the hills of Montana walks 12 miles, one way, to the general store.

"Heya, Wilbur," says Sam, the store owner. "Tell me, are you and Myrtle still making fires up there by rubbing stones and flint together?"

"You betcha, Sam. Ain't no 'tother way. Why?" says the cowboy.

"Got something to show you," says the Sam. "Something to make fire. It's called a match."

"Match? Never heard of it."

"Watch this. If you want a fire, you just do this," Sam says, taking a match and striking it on his pants.

"Huh. Well, that's somethin', but that ain't for me, Sam."

"Well, why not?"

"I can't be walkin' 12 miles to borrow your pants every time I wants a fire."

It's All in the Message

Cowboy Wisdom

When you're throwin' your weight around, be ready to have it thrown around by somebody else.

Cowboy Joe lived on a quiet rural highway. But as time went by, the traffic slowly built up at an alarming rate. The traffic was so heavy and so fast that his chickens were being run over at a rate of three to six per day.

So one day Cowboy Joe calls the sheriff's office and says, "You've got to do something about all of these people driving so fast and killing my chickens."

"What do you want me to do?" asks the sheriff.

"I don't care. Just do something about those crazy drivers!"

The next day, the sheriff orders the county workers to go out and erect a sign that says, "Slow—School Crossing."

Three days later, Cowboy Joe calls the sheriff and says, "You've got to do something about these drivers. The 'School Crossing' sign seems to make 'em go even faster."

Again, the sheriff sends out the county workers, and they put up a new sign: "Slow: Children at Play."

That sign seems to really speed up the drivers, so Cowboy Joe calls the sheriff every day for three weeks. Finally, he says to the sheriff, "Yer signs are doing no good. Can I put up my own sign?"

The sheriff says to him, "Sure thing, put up your own sign." He is willing to let Cowboy Joe do just about anything to stop him from calling every day to complain.

The sheriff receives no more calls from Cowboy Joe. Three weeks later, curiosity gets the best of the sheriff, and he phones Cowboy Joe and asks, "How's the problem with those drivers? Did you put up your sign?"

"Oh, I sure did. And not one chicken has been killed since I put up that sign. I've got to go. I'm very busy," says Cowboy Joe before he hangs up the phone.

The sheriff is really curious about the sign now, and he says to himself, "I'd better go out there and take a look at that sign—it might be something that we can use to slow down drivers."

The sheriff drives out to Cowboy Joe's house, and his jaw drops the moment he sees the sign. The words are spray-painted on a sheet of wood: "Nudist Colony. Go Slow, and Watch Out for the Chicks."

Moose Hunting

Two cowboys from Utah fly to a remote lake in Alaska to hunt moose. They have a good hunt, and both manage to bag large moose. When the plane returns to pick them up, the pilot looks at the animals and says, "This little plane won't lift all of us, the equipment and both those moose. You'll have to leave one. We'll never make it over the trees on takeoff."

"That's baloney!" says one of the cowboys.

> Q: Who is the laziest cowboy in the Wild West?
>
> A: The Stoned Ranger.

"Yeah," the other agrees, "you're just chicken. We came out here last year and got two moose, and that pilot had some guts! He wasn't afraid to take off!"

"Yeah," says the first cowboy, "and his plane wasn't any bigger than yours!"

The pilot gets angry and says, "Hell, if he did it, then I can do it! I can fly as well as anybody!"

They load up the plane, taxi at full throttle and the plane almost makes it, but it doesn't clear the trees at the end of the lake. The plane clips the treetops, flips, then breaks up, scattering the baggage, animal carcasses and passengers all through the brush.

Still alive, but hurt and dazed, the pilot sits up, shakes his head to clear it, and says, "Where are we?"

One of the cowboys rolls out from under a bush, looks around and says, "I'd say about 100 yards farther than last year."

Chapter Five

Say What?

School Boy

A boy from Wyoming rushes home from kindergarten and tells his mother, "I need a set of pistols, a gun belt and a holster."

"Why would you need those things?" asks the mother. "Surely you don't need them for school?"

"I do, Mom," says the boy. "Teacher says tomorrow she's going to teach us to draw."

Misunderstanding

Young cowboy: "I went shooting with my pa yesterday."

Young girl: "What did ya git?"

Young cowboy: "Four rabbits and a potfer."

Young girl: "What's a potfer?"

Young cowboy: "Why fer cooking the rabbits, silly!"

Where Y'all From?

A police officer sees a man dressed as a cowboy in the street, complete with a huge Stetson hat, spurs and six-shooters. "Excuse me, sir," says the police officer, "who are you?"

"My name's Tex, officer," replies the cowboy.

"What?" says the police officer. "Are you from Texas?"

"Nope, Louisiana."

"Louisiana? So why are you called Tex?"

"Don't want to be called Louise, now do I?"

Horse Whisperer

A cowboy in the Old West is captured by a tribe of fierce Indians, but considering themselves somewhat civilized, they grant the cowboy three wishes before they kill him.

Considering his situation carefully, the cowboy says, "For my first wish, I'd like to talk to my horse."

So the Indians bring his horse, and the cowboy whispers into the horse's ear. The loyal animal almost seems to nod its head, then trots off and returns an hour later with a beautiful blonde woman on its back.

The cowboy is clearly upset and says, "For my second wish, I want to talk to my horse again."

The Indians are perplexed, but they grant this wish as well. Again, the cowboy whispers in his horse's ear, and again the animal trots off, returning an hour later with a beautiful redhead on its back. The cowboy fumes, throws his hat on the ground and stomps on it.

The Indians inquire as to the cowboy's final wish, and he says, "Let me talk to my horse one more time." The cowboy whispers into the horse's ear. The animal nods, trots off and returns an hour later with a beautiful brunette on its back.

Q: Who was the first skeleton to haunt the Wild West?

A: The Bone Ranger.

Furious, the cowboys shouts, "You stupid horse! I said *posse*!"

Tea Time

Englishman: "All right, mate! Fancy a tea or coffee?"
Indian: "Tee-pees."

The End

Stanley owns the biggest spread in Nevada. After a long life of ranching, the 83-year-old knows that the time has come for him to head for his last roundup. His four adult children are gathered around Stanley's deathbed.

As he seems to doze off into a blissful sleep, Stanley's progeny begin discussing funeral plans.

One wants to spend $100 for a coffin, a second thinks a plain wooden box will do and the third is even ready to dump the old man's remains into a paper bag.

All of Stanley's children agree that there is no reason to spend much money because their father will never know the difference.

Just then, Stanley stirs. Having heard every word, he thinks it is time to set the record straight. "Youngin's," he says, "I've never told y'all this and never wanted to, but I can't go to my final restin' place a-carryin' this with me. My dear children, your mother and I were never married."

Stanley's eldest son is aghast. "You mean we're…"

The old man glares at him and says, "Yup. And cheap ones, too!"

Nightmare

Pecos Bill and his pardner Andy are slugging down beers at the Last Gasp Saloon. After lighting the stub of a cigar, Andy turns to Bill and says, "Pecos, ya know, I had the worst dream of my life last night—a real nightmare. I dreamed I was with 12 of the purttiest chorus girls in the world. Blondes, brunettes, redheads, all dancin' in a row."

Bill says, "Now, hold on thar a sec, cowpoke. That don't sound so turrible tuh me."

"Oh yeah? I was the third girl from the end."

The Beat Goes On

A group of cowboys are relaxing around a campfire when they hear the sound of distant drums. With a grim look on his face, one of the cowboys remarks, "I don't like the sound of them drums…"

Suddenly, an Indian jumps out from behind a nearby rock and replies, "That's okay—he's not our usual drummer."

Everything Is Big in Texas

A Texan sitting in a restaurant notices a gorgeous woman sitting alone at another table. He calls the waiter over and asks for the most expensive bottle of champagne to be sent over to her, knowing that if she accepts it, she is his.

The waiter gets the bottle and quickly takes it over to the woman, telling her it's from the gentleman.

The woman looks at the champagne, writes a note and sends it with the bottle back over to the Texan.

The note reads: "For me to accept this bottle, you need to have a Mercedes in your garage, $1 million in the bank and seven inches in your pants."

Well, the Texan, after reading the note, sends his own note back to her, and it reads: "Just so you know, I happen to have *two* Mercedes in my garage, and I have over *$2 million* in the bank, but not even for *you* would I cut off two inches! Sorry, honey."

Kids!

A Southern schoolboy is studying Greek mythology. When the teacher asks him to name something that was half-man and half-beast, the boy replies, "Buffalo Bill."

Blowin' in the Wind

A broke and dirty cowboy walks into a bar and says, "Gimme a whiskey."

The bartender says, "I'll have to see your money first."

"I'm broke, but if ya give me a bottle of whiskey, I'll get up on that stage and fart 'Dixie'!"

The bartender has never seen someone fart any kind of song, so he agrees.

The cowboy drinks the whole bottle of whiskey then staggers up on stage. The customers in the bar start applauding. He drops his pants, and the people in the bar start cheering even louder. Then he bends over and craps all over the stage. Everyone is disgusted and gets up to leave.

Q: Where do most Mormon horses live?

A: Salt Lick City!

The bartender screams, "You said you were gonna fart 'Dixie,' not crap all over my stage!"

The cowboy replies, "Hey! Even Frank Sinatra had to clear his throat before he sang!"

Cowboy on the Train

A beautiful woman is sitting on a train. There is an empty seat next to her. A cowboy dressed in a Stetson hat and fancy cowboy boots saunters over and says, "Pardon me, ma'am, do ya mind if I sit here?"

The woman looks up at him and says, "I most certainly do! Cowboys are disgusting! I hate cowboys! Cowboys are mean, crude, vile and uncouth! I'll tell you something else I know about cowboys. Cowboys will screw anything! Cowboys will screw sheep, they'll screw cattle, they'll screw dogs, they'll screw lizards, they'll screw chickens…"

The incredulous cowboy remarks, "Chickens?"

Herd of Cows

A young man from interior British Columbia is visiting a dude ranch and wants to appear macho, so he goes out walking with one of the hired hands. As they are walking through the barnyard, the visitor tries starting a conversation. "Say, look at that big bunch of cows."

The hired hand replies, "Not *bunch—herd*."

"Heard what?"

"*Herd* of cows."

"Sure, I've heard of cows. There's a big bunch of 'em right over there."

Chokin'!

Ed and Ken, two cowboys from Arizona, walk into a roadhouse bar to have a beer to wash the trail dust from their throats. They stand at the bar, drinking their beers and talking quietly about cattle prices. Suddenly, a woman eating a sandwich at a table behind them begins to cough. After a moment, it becomes apparent that she is in real distress, and the cowboys turn to look at her.

"Kin ya swaller?" asks Ken.

The woman shakes her head.

"Kin ya breathe?" asks Ed.

The woman, beginning to turn a bit blue, shakes her head again.

> **Q:** What young cowboy terrorizes kids all day?
>
> **A:** Bully the Kid.

Ken walks up behind her, lifts up the back of her skirt, yanks down her panties and slowly runs his tongue from the back of her thigh up to the small of her back. This shocks the woman so much that she erupts into a violent spasm, the obstruction flies out of her mouth and she begins to breathe again.

The cowboys walk back over to the bar and take a swig of beer.

Ed says, "Ya know, I'd heard of that there Hind Lick maneuver, but I never seen anybody do it."

Speed of What?

Four old cowboys are having a discussion about what is the fastest thing in the world.

The first cowboy says, "I believe it's thinking, 'cuz when you prick your finger or touch a flame, the pain instantly becomes thought and hits the brain."

The second cowboy says, "Well, I think it's blinking. When you blink and open your eyes again, you immediately see everything. Nothing is changed."

The third cowboy says, "Well, I think it's light, 'cuz as soon as you press that light switch, you go from dark to instant light."

The fourth cowboy says, "Well, I think it's the Mexican two-step diarrhea."

All the others say simultaneously, "Diarrhea? Why?"

The fourth cowboy says, "I'll explain it to you. I went across the border to a saloon last night and drank a buncha homemade Mexican tequila. On the way home from the saloon, I stopped off at Maria's Cafe and ate two helpings of her Mexican Special, which had been warmed over a time or two, with a buncha jalapenos and some chili peppers I never saw before."

The first cowboy asks, "So, what's that got to do with speed or diarrhea?"

Cowboy Wisdom
The easiest way to eat crow is while it's still warm. The colder it gets, the harder it is to swaller.

The fourth cowboy says, "Well, later on when I was in bed, I felt this sudden fire and a fierce rumbling in my belly, and before I could think, blink or turn that damn light on...I shit myself."

Look-a-like

Outlaw: "I'm going to shoot you!"

Sheriff: "Why?"

Outlaw: "Because I shoot anyone who looks like me."

Sheriff: "And I look like you?"

Outlaw: "Yes."

Sheriff: "Then shoot me, please!"

Bull Fight

A big cowboy stops at a local restaurant following a day of drinking and roaming around in Mexico. While sipping his tequila, he notices a sizzling, scrumptious-looking platter of food being served at the next table.

Not only does the food look good, but the smell is wonderful.

He asks the waiter, "What is that you just served?"

Cowboys refer to beans as "Deceitful Beans" because sometimes they talk behind your back.

The waiter replies, "Ah señor, you have excellent taste! Those are bull's testicles from the bullfight this morning. A delicacy!"

The cowboy, though momentarily daunted, says, "What the heck, I'm on vacation down here! Bring me an order!"

The waiter replies, "I am so sorry, señor. There is only one serving per day because there is only one bullfight each morning. If you come early tomorrow and place your order, we will be sure to save you this delicacy!"

The next morning, the cowboy returns and places his order, and that evening he is served the one and only special delicacy of the day.

After taking a few bites and inspecting the contents of his platter, he calls over the waiter and says, "These are delicious, but they are much, much smaller than the ones I saw you serve yesterday."

The waiter shrugs his shoulders and says, "Si, señor. Sometimes the bull wins."

Ladies Night at the Saloon

A blonde, a brunette and a redhead walk into a saloon and order drinks from the barkeep.

Brunette: "I'll have a B and C."

Bartender: "What is a B and C?".

Brunette: "Bourbon and Coke."

Redhead: "And I'll have a G and T."

Bartender: "What's a G and T?"

Redhead: "Gin and tonic."

Blonde: "I'll have a 15."

Bartender: "What's a 15?"

Blonde: "Seven and Seven."

Cowboy Logic

The Sierra Club and the U.S. Forest Service are presenting an alternative to Wyoming sheep ranchers for controlling the coyote population. It seems that after years of the ranchers using the tried-and-true methods of shooting and/or trapping the predator, the tree-huggers have a more "humane" solution.

Cowboy Wisdom

If you be leadin' someone around by his nose, it don't say much about him, and it says even less about you.

One of the tree-huggers proposes that the animals be captured alive and the males be castrated and then let loose again, which would control the coyote population.

All of the ranchers thought it was an amazing idea—for a couple of minutes. Finally, an old boy in the back stands up, tips his hat back and says, "Son, I don't think you understand the problem. Those coyotes ain't screwin' our sheep—they're eatin' 'em."

Priest and the Donkey

A priest who wants to raise money for his church is told there is a future in horse racing. He decides to purchase a horse and enter it in the races. However, at the local auction, the going price for a horse is so steep that he ends up buying a donkey instead. He figures since he has the donkey, he might just as well enter it in the race. To his surprise, the donkey comes in third. The next day, the racing sheet carries the headline, "Priest's Ass Shows."

The priest is pleased with the donkey's performance and enters it in the races again. This time, the donkey wins. The paper the next day reads, "Priest's Ass Out Front."

The bishop is so upset with this kind of publicity that he orders the priest not to enter the donkey in any more races. The newspaper reads, "Bishop Scratches Priest's Ass."

This is just too much for the bishop, and he orders the priest to get rid of the donkey. The priest gives the donkey to a nun at a nearby convent, and the newspaper headline reads, "Nun Has Best Ass in Town."

Upon reading this, the bishop faints. After he recovers from the shock, he informs the nun that she has to dispose of the donkey. She sells it to a farmer for $10. The paper states, "Nun Peddles Ass for Ten Bucks."

The bishop is buried the next day.

Meeting the Mayor

A cowboy attends a social function where the mayor is trying to gather support for his new campaign. Once he discovers there is a cowboy in the room, the mayor starts to belittle him by talking in a southern drawl and using single-syllable words.

As he is doing that, the mayor keeps swatting at flies buzzing around his head. The cowboy says, "Y'all havin' some problem with them circle flies?"

The mayor stops talking and says, "Well, yes, if that's what they're called, but I've never heard of 'circle flies.'"

"Well, sir," the cowboy replies, "circle flies hang around ranches. They're called circle flies because they're almost always found circling around the back end of a horse."

"Oh," the mayor replies as he goes back to his rambling. But a moment later, he stops and bluntly asks, "Are you calling me a horse's ass?"

"No, sir," the cowboy replies, "I have too much respect for the citizens of this county to call their mayor a horse's ass."

"That's a good thing," the mayor responds.

After a long pause, the cowboy says, "Hard to fool them flies, though."

Train Robbery

Cowboy Wisdom
Never smack a man who's chewing tobacco.

A business banker is on a train in the Old West. He really has to take a dump, but there are no bathrooms on the train. He decides that since there is no one else in the car with him, he can just relieve himself out the window.

At the same time, two bandits are walking along the tracks. One looks up and says to the other, "Hey, you see that ugly guy hanging out the window? When the train goes by, I'll smack his face, and you grab that cigar!"

Old-timer

Back in cowboy times, pioneers on a westbound wagon train are lost and low on food. They haven't seen any other humans for days, but one day the pioneers come across an old man sitting beneath a tree.

Q: Why did the cowboy get a hot seat?

A: Because he rode the range.

"Is there some place ahead where we can get food?" asks one of the pioneers.

"Vell, I tink so," the old man says in a thick German accent, "but I vouldn't go up dat hill und down de udder side. Somevun tolt me you'd run into a big bacon tree."

"A bacon tree?" says the wagon train leader.

"Yah, a bacon tree. Vould I lie? Trust me. I vouldn't go dere."

The leader goes back and tells his people what the old German man said.

"So why did he say not to go there?" asks one of the pioneers.

Another pioneer says, "Oh, you know those old-timers—they lie just for a joke."

So the leader decides to take the wagon up the hill and down the other side. Suddenly, Indians attack the group and massacre everyone except the leader, who manages to escape and goes back to the old man.

Near dead, the leader shouts, "You old fool! You sent us to our deaths! We followed the route, but there was no bacon tree—just hundreds of Indians who killed everyone but me."

The old man holds up his hand and says, "Vait a minute." He picks up an English-German dictionary and begins quickly thumbing through it. "Oy, I made such ah big mishtake! It vuzn't a bacon tree…it vuz a ham bush."

Butcher

A cowboy walks into a butcher's shop and asks the butcher, "Are you a gambling man?"

The butcher says, "Yes."

So the cowboy says, "I bet you $50 that you can't reach up and touch that meat hanging on the hooks up there."

The butcher says, "I'm not betting on that."

"But I thought you were a gambling man!" the cowboy retorts.

"Yes, I am," replies the butcher. "But the steaks are too high."

Learning

A man and his son recently move to Wyoming. One Saturday afternoon they decide to take a walk through a local park. During the walk, the boy sees two cowboys stroll by.

"Dad, look at those bow-legged bastards!"

The father is surprised by this and tells his son not to use such bad language.

A few minutes later, two more cowboys walk by, and again the boy yells, "Dad, look at those bow-legged bastards!"

The father, quite upset now, turns to his son and says, "I told you not to say that, and I do not want to hear it again, or else!"

Just a few minutes pass by, and another pair of cowboys cross their path, and once again the son yells, "Dad, look at those bow-legged bastards!"

"That's it!" the father yells. He takes the boy home and locks him in his room with the complete works of Shakespeare to teach him a lesson about language.

Two weeks later, the father notices that his son has taken to speaking like Shakespeare wrote. This impresses the father so he decides to take his son out for another walk through the park. As they are walking, a pair of cowboys walk past them.

Cowboy Wisdom
Never ask how stupid someone is 'cuz they'll turn around and show you.

The boy turns to his father and says, "Father, what strange men are these whose balls hang in parentheses!"

Lottery

A cowboy wins the lottery. He goes to Winnipeg to claim his winnings, and the clerk verifies his ticket number. The cowboy says, "I want my $20 million."

The clerk replies, "No, sir. It doesn't work that way. We give you one million today, and then you'll get the rest spread out for the next 19 years."

The cowboy says, "Oh, no! I want all my money right now! I won it, and I want it all."

Again, the clerk explains that he will only get one million that day and the rest during the next 19 years.

The cowboy, furious with the clerk, screams out, "Look, I want my money! If you're not going to give me my $20 million right now, then I want my dollar back!"

Smart Cowboy

Jett is trying to light a match. He strikes the first one, and it doesn't work, so he throws it away.

He strikes the second match. That doesn't work either, so he tosses it.

Jett strikes a third match, and it lights up.

"That's a good one!" says the cowboy to himself, blowing it out. "Ah'm gonna save it!"

Hallucinations

After being lost in the bush for a week, a cowboy is miraculously found alive, but he is convinced that he is dead, and nobody, it seems, can persuade him otherwise. When his family can't help him, a psychiatrist is called in. For three days, the psychiatrist talks to the cowboy, trying to convince him that he inhabits the world of the living. Finally, the doctor gets the cowboy to agree to one point—dead men don't bleed.

"Now," says the psychiatrist, "I will prick your finger with a needle." He does so, and the cowboy's finger starts to bleed.

"What does that tell you?" asks the psychiatrist triumphantly.

"That dead men *do* bleed!"

In Church

A Montana cowboy returns home from church with two black eyes. "What on earth happened to you?" asks his wife.

"Well, I was sitting there in church and I noticed the woman in front of me had her dress sticking in her crack. I reached over the pew and pulled it out, then she turned around and punched me in the eye.

"Okay. That explains the one black eye, but about the other one?" asks his wife.

"Well, I figured that must have been how she wanted her dress, so I put it back."

Drunk Man

Near closing time at a country bar, an old cowboy falls off his stool and can't get back up. Watching him struggle to stand on his own two feet, a stranger takes pity on the poor drunk and offers to drive him home. The cowboy is so drunk that he has to be dragged to the car. When they arrive at the cowboy's home, the stranger then has to drag him to the front steps. The cowboy's wife opens the front door.

"I had to bring your husband home from the bar," explains the stranger, "because I'm afraid he can't even stand up, let alone walk."

"I understand," says the wife. "But tell me, where's his wheelchair?"

Momma

A drunk cowboy is staggering down a road when he sees a woman walking with a young child.

"Lady," says the cowboy, "that is the ugliest kid I've ever seen in my life. It's uglier than a newborn baby pig."

As the drunk wanders off down the dusty road, the woman bursts into tears.

Another cowboy walking by notices she is crying and says, "What's the matter, ma'am?"

"I've just been terribly insulted!" she cries.

Q: Why do outlaws have to be strong?

A: Because they hold up banks.

121

"There, there," says the cowboy. "Take this tissue and wipe your tears, and here is a banana for your hairless chimp."

Jones the . . .

A young man wanders into a small New Mexico town and gets to talking to an old cowboy named Bill Jones. After a while, the old man begins to vent his frustrations.

"See that row of houses over there?" he says. "I built 'em all, but do they call me Jones the Builder? No, they damn well don't! See that railroad line? I laid it, but do they call me Jones the Engineer? No, they damn well don't! But years ago, I sleep with just one sheep, and…"

Misunderstanding

Cowboy Wisdom

If you get to thinkin' you're a person of some influence, try orderin' somebody else's dog around.

A rancher walks into the local tavern and sits down at the bar.

The rancher mumbles, "Some things I just can't explain."

The bartender, who knows the man as Jim, asks, "What do you mean, Jim?"

"Well, you know my old cow, Betsy? I was milkin' her this mornin', and out of the blue, she knocks the pail of milk over with her right back leg. So I pick up a piece of rope layin' nearby and cut me off a piece. I tied her right leg to the nearby post, but some things I just can't explain," replies Jim.

"What can't you explain?" asks the bartender.

"Well, I commenced to milkin' her again, and when the pail got half full, Betsy kicked it over with her left back leg. So I took the leftover piece of rope and tied her left leg to another post, but some things I just can't explain," adds Jim.

"Jim, tell me what it is you can't explain, and I'll see if I can help," says the bartender.

Jim says, "Well, after that I went back to milkin' her again, I got the pail half full, and I'll be darned if Betsy didn't knock the pail over with her tail. Since I didn't have any more rope left, I took off my belt and tied one end to her tail. Then I stood up on my stool and reached up to hook the belt buckle on a nail just above. About that time, my pants fell to my ankles, and my wife walks into the barn. That's what I can't explain."

Q: How does an Indian indicate that he is about to make a turn on his horse?

A: He uses smoke signals.

Cowboys on a Bus

A bus stops and two southern cowboys get on. They sit down and engage in an animated conversation. The woman sitting behind them ignores them at first, but her attention is galvanized when she hears one of the men say, "Emma come first. Den I come. Den two asses come together. I come once mo'. Two asses, they come together again. I come again and pee twice. Den I come one last time."

"You foul-mouthed sex-obsessed swine!" retorts the woman indignantly. "In this country, we don't speak aloud in public places about our sex lives!"

123

"Hey, cool down, ma'am," says the man. "Who's talkin' 'bout sex? I'm jus' tellin' ma friend how to spell Mississippi."

Whiskey Drinker

A fancy-dressed man walks into a cowboy bar and orders a glass of 12-year-old scotch.

The bartender, believing that the man will not be able to tell the difference, pours him a shot of the cheap three-year-old house scotch that has been poured into an empty bottle of the good stuff.

Cowboy Wisdom
Alcohol is not the answer—it makes you forget the question.

The man takes a sip, spits the scotch out on the bar and reams the bartender. "This is the cheapest three-year-old scotch you can buy! I'm not paying for it. Now, give me a good 12-year-old scotch."

The bartender, now feeling a bit of a challenge, pours the man a scotch of much better quality—six-year-old scotch. The man takes a sip and spits it out on the bar. "This is only six-year-old scotch. I won't pay for this, and I insist on a good, 12-year-old scotch."

The bartender finally relents and serves the man his best-quality, 12-year-old scotch. The man sips the drink and says, "Now that's more like it."

A cowboy sitting at the end of the bar has witnessed the entire episode and walks up to the finicky scotch drinker and sets a glass down in front of him and says, "What do ya think of this?"

The scotch expert takes a sip, and in disgust, violently spits out the liquid yelling, "This tastes like piss!"

The cowboy replies, "That's right. Now guess how old I am."

Wayne, John Wayne

John Wayne walks into a saloon. Everybody stops drinking, and an uneasy silence fills the bar. Everyone in the room is aware that the most dangerous, deadliest, toughest, fastest gun in the West has just walked in the room, and they all get out of his way.

John sits at the bar and orders himself a whiskey. The cowboy next to him tries to stay cool, but he begins to shake.

John notices and says, "Two plus two?"

The cowboy is so scared that he can hardly get a word out. He manages to say, "What?"

John looks at him with contempt and repeats, "Two plus two. Answer me now!"

The cowboy is completely terrified and blurts out, "Five!"

Within the blink of an eye, John shoots him dead, puts his gun back in his holster and orders another whiskey.

The bartender, shocked, asks, "Excuse me, Mr. Wayne, but why did you shoot him?"

John knocks back his whiskey, looks at the bartender and says, "He knew too much."

Challenge

A cowboy walks into a Louisiana bar and notices that a contest is going on.

The bartender tells him the details. "First, you have to drink three bottles of moonshine. Second, you go out back and pull a sore tooth out of the mouth of my pet gator. And finally, you have to go upstairs and have sex with Ma

> **Cowboy Wisdom**
> Timing has a lot to do with the outcome of a rain dance.

Jackson, the town's oldest and ugliest prostitute. If you can do all that in one hour and stay conscious, you win a year's supply of beer."

"Sounds tough," says the cowboy, "but I'll give it a try."

Q: What is the best selling Wild West food in the Chinese take away?

A: Won Tonto soup.

The cowboy drinks three bottles of moonshine, then, completely plastered, staggers out back to find the gator. After half an hour of crashes and screaming, the man crawls back into the bar covered in bruises and cuts. "Okay," slurs the cowboy, "sho where ish the old broad with the bad tooth?"

Another Drunk

A drunk cowboy is sitting in a bar. He asks the bartender, "Where's the bathroom at?" The bartender says, "Go down the hall and make a right."

The cowboy heads down the hall and, all of a sudden, everybody at the bar hears a loud scream coming from the bathroom, and they wonder what's going on in there. A few minutes go by, and again, everybody at the bar hears another loud scream coming out of the bathroom. This time, the bartender goes to investigate.

"What's all the screaming about in here?" says the bartender. "You're scaring all my customers away."

The drunk cowboy whines, "I'm sitting on the toilet, and every time I go to flush it, something comes up and squeezes the heck out of my gonads!"

The bartender opens the bathroom door and says, "No wonder! You're sitting on a mop bucket, you idiot!"

Tribal Death

Three cowboys are captured by a tribe in South Dakota. The chief is going to punish the intruders for trespassing on their land. He calls the first cowboy to the front of the tribe and asks, "Death or Booka?"

The cowboy doesn't want to die, so he opts for Booka. The tribe starts screaming 'Booka!' and dancing around. The chief rips the cowboy's pants off and has sex with him.

The chief calls the second cowboy to step forward and asks, "Death or Booka?" Well, not wanting to die either, the cowboy opts for Booka. The tribe again starts screaming 'Booka!' and dancing around. The chief rips the second guy's pants off and has sex with him.

The chief calls the third cowboy to the front and asks, "Death or Booka?"

The third cowboy has a little more self-respect and thinks death would be better than being violated in such a way, so he opts for death.

The chief turns to the tribe and screams, "Death by Booka!"

Satan

One bright, beautiful Sunday morning, everyone in the tiny town of Johnstown, Tennessee, gets up early and goes to the local church.

Before the services start, the townspeople sit in the pews and talk about their lives, their families and work.

Suddenly, Satan appears at the front of the church.

Everyone starts screaming and running for the entrance, trampling each other in a frantic effort to get away from evil incarnate.

Soon, the church is empty, except for one elderly cowboy who sits calmly in his pew, not moving and seemingly oblivious to the fact that God's ultimate enemy is in his presence.

Now, this confuses Satan a bit, so he walks up to the cowboy and says, "Don't you know who I am?"

Cowboy Wisdom
You don't have to step in a cow pie to know what crap smells like.

The man replies, "Yep, sure do."

Satan asks, "Aren't you afraid of me?"

"Nope, sure ain't," says the cowboy.

Satan is a little perturbed at this and says, "Why aren't you afraid of me?"

The cowboy calmly replies, "Been married to your sister for over 48 years."

Stranded

A cowboy is stranded out in the Arizona desert when his truck breaks down. He walks in the heat and dust for an hour until he notices something moving off in the distance. The cowboy quickens his pace and discovers a yard full of children playing.

The man calls out to a woman on the front porch, "Ma'am, do you have a monkey wrench?"

"Dis ain't no monkey ranch, dese my children!"

Signals

A cowboy is traveling through an Indian reservation in Arizona when he stops for a coffee. He sits at the table, lights up a cigar and quietly blows smoke rings.

After he blows about 10 rings into the air, an angry Indian man comes up to him and says, "Listen, buddy, if you don't stop calling me names, I'll smash your face in!"

Confession

A drunk cowboy staggers into a Catholic church, enters a confessional box and sits down but says nothing. The priest coughs a few times to get the man's attention, but the drunk just sits there without saying a word. Finally, the priest pounds three times on the wall.

The drunk mumbles, "Ain't no use knockin'—ain't no paper on this side either."

CHAPTER SIX

Life, Death and Cowboy Justice

A Hangin'!

> **Q:** Why does everyone hate the cowboy at the fairground?
>
> **A:** He keeps setting six shots at everything.

Back in the Old West, three cowboys are about to be hanged for cattle rustling. The lynch mob takes the three men to a tree right at the edge of the Rio Grande. The idea is that when each man has died, they will cut the rope and the body will drop into the river and drift out of sight.

They put the first cowboy in the noose, but he is so sweaty and greasy that he slips out, falls in the river and swims to freedom.

The mob ties the noose around the second cowboy's neck. He, too, slips out of the rope, drops into the river and gets away.

As they drag the third cowboy to the scaffold, he resists. "Please! Would y'all tighten that noose a little bit? I can't swim!"

Where's My Hoss?

A cowboy rides into a town and stops at a saloon for a drink. Unfortunately, the locals have a habit of picking on strangers. When he finishes his drink, he leaves the saloon and finds that his horse has been stolen. He goes back into the bar, and with a quick flash of his hands, he flips his guns into the air, catches them above his head and without looking, fires a warning shot into the ceiling.

> **Cowboy Wisdom**
> Good judgment comes from experience, and a lot of that comes from bad judgment.

"Which one of you varmints stole my hoss?" yells the cowboy. No one answers.

"All right, I'm gonna have another beer, and if my hoss ain't back outside by the time I finish, I'm gonna do what I done did in Red Deer! And I don't like to do what I done in Red Deer!"

Scared for their lives, the thieves run out of the bar to retrieve the cowboy's horse.

Curious, the bartender looks at the cowboy and says, "You have to tell me what happened in Red Deer."

"Awww, nuthin' really. I had to walk back, and I hate that!"

Gomer

The local sheriff is looking for a deputy, so Gomer, who is not exactly the sharpest knife in the drawer, applies for the job.

"Okay," the sheriff drawls, "Gomer, what is one and one?"

"Eleven," he replies.

The sheriff thinks to himself, *That's not what I meant, but in one way he's right.*

"What two days of the week start with the letter 'T'?"

"Today and tomorrow," says Gomer.

The sheriff is again surprised that Gomer gives a correct answer that the lawman never thought of himself.

"Now, Gomer, listen carefully. Who killed Abraham Lincoln?"

Gomer looks a little surprised then thinks really hard for a minute and finally says, "I don't know."

"Well, why don't you go home and work on that one for a while?"

Q: Why did the sheriff arrest the crow?

A: It was caught making crank caws!

Gomer wanders over to the barbershop where his pals are waiting to hear the results of the interview.

Gomer is exultant. "It went great! First day on the job and I'm already working on a murder case!"

Brown Paper Man

A sheriff walks into a saloon and gives a holler for everyone's attention. "Has anyone seen Brown Paper Jake?" he asks.

"What's he look like?" asks one shoddy-looking cowboy.

"Well," replies the sheriff, "he's sportin' a brown paper hat, wears a brown paper waistcoat, brown paper shirt, brown paper jacket, brown paper pants and brown paper boots."

"So what's he wanted for?" asks the same cowboy.

"Rustlin'," replies the lawman.

School?

A nasty-looking hombre walks into the Dodge City bank and produces a silver-plated six-shooter. He points the gun at the teller and says, "Gimme all the loot, pardner, or youse'll be geography."

The shaken teller looks up and says, "Don't you mean *history*?"

The robber replies, "Don't change the subject!"

Death Row

A cowboy and a biker are on death row and are scheduled to be executed on the same day. When that day comes, they are taken out to the gas chamber. The warden turns to the cowboy and asks if he has any last requests.

> **Cowboy Wisdom**
> If you find yourself in a hole, the first thing to do is stop diggin'.

The cowboy replies, "Ah shor do, warden. Ah'd be mighty grateful if you'd play 'Achy Breaky Heart' for me before I hafta go."

"Sure, we can do that," says the warden. "How about you, biker, what's your last request?"

"That you kill me first!"

Preacher Man

One Sunday a cowboy goes to church. When he enters, he sees that he and the preacher are the only people present. The preacher asks the cowboy if he wants him to go ahead and preach.

The cowboy says, "I ain't too smart, but if I went to feed my cattle and only one showed up, I'd feed him." So the minister begins his sermon.

One hour passes by, then two hours, then two-and-a-half hours. The preacher finally finishes his sermon and asks the cowboy how he liked the sermon.

The cowboy answers slowly, "Well, I ain't very smart, but if I went to feed my cattle and only one showed up, I sure wouldn't feed him all the hay."

Death Row Inmates

A German, an Italian and a cowboy are on death row. The warden gives them a choice of three ways to die: 1) to be shot, 2) to be hung, or 3) to be injected with the AIDS virus for a slow death.

The German says, "Shoot me right in the head." Boom! He dies instantly.

The Italian says, "Just hang me." Snap! He dies quickly.

Then the cowboy says, "Gimme some of that AIDS stuff."

The warden gives him the injection, and the cowboy falls down laughing. The warden and the guards look at each other and wonder what is wrong with this guy.

Then the cowboy says, "Give me another one of those shots." So the warden does.

Now the cowboy is laughing so hard that tears roll from his eyes, and he doubles over.

Finally, the warden says, "What is wrong with you?"

The cowboy replies, "You guys are so stupid! I'm wearin' a condom!"

Cowboy Mystery

A man lives next door to a cowboy. The man constantly hears a strange noise coming from the cowboy's house. At first, he tries to just ignore it. But after a while he just can't take it, so he goes and knocks on the cowboy's door.

The cowboy opens the door and says, "Yes, can I help you?"

The man says, "I'd like to know what that noise coming from your house is."

The cowboy replies, "I'm sorry. I can't tell you. You're not a cowboy."

The man says, "How do I become a cowboy then?"

"Well, to start, you must go the next five years eating only steak," says the cowboy.

So the man, determined to find out what that noise is, goes home and spends the next five years eating only steak. Finally, he returns to the cowboy and says, "Okay, it's been five years, and I've only eaten steak. Now can I know what that noise is?"

> **Q:** What sickness do cowboys get from riding wild horses?
>
> **A:** Bronc-hitis

The cowboy replies, "No, you're still not a cowboy. Now you must drink nothing but whiskey for seven years."

Well, the man isn't looking forward to waiting seven more years, but as he has already put in five years and is determined to find the source of that noise, he goes home and drinks nothing but whiskey for seven years. When finally he reaches the end of those seven long years, he once again returns to the cowboy and says, "It's been seven years, and I've drank nothing but whiskey, now can I find out what that noise is?"

The cowboy says, "No, you're still not a cowboy. Now we must test your faith. Go to the highest cliff in the area and jump off."

Well, the man has come this far, and he isn't going to back down, so he goes to the highest cliff and jumps. Luckily, there was a safety net at the bottom of the cliff, and he survives. When he climbs back up the cliff, the cowboy is waiting for him.

The cowboy leads him back to his house and says, "You have passed the tests. You are now a cowboy. I assume you now wish to know what causes the noise you have been hearing?"

The man replies, "Oh God, yes! I've waited over 12 years to find out."

The cowboy gestures for him to follow and leads him down the stairs into the basement. Once in the basement, the cowboy opens a door that leads into a tunnel. The cowboy tells the man to go to the end of the tunnel.

Q: What do you get when you cross a goat, a donkey and a ram?

A: Simple—a hard kick in the Aaaaaass.

The man starts walking down the tunnel, and it goes on for a long way, but finally he reaches the end. There is only one more door between him and the source of the noise. He grabs the doorknob, turns it and opens the door. In the room he sees—I'm sorry, I can't tell you what he saw. You're not a cowboy!

Dead Man

Two cowboys are carrying their dead friend to the undertaker. "He was the fastest gun in Kansas," says one of the cowboys.

"Too bad he was in Arizona," says the other.

Gamblin' Man

In a dark, smoke-filled saloon, a group of dangerous cowboys are sitting around a table playing a game of high-stakes poker. These are serious games with serious men who are known for their itchy trigger fingers should anyone get out of line or even look at someone cross-eyed.

> **Cowboy Wisdom**
> Just 'cuz trouble comes visitin' doesn't mean you have to offer it a place to sit down.

It just so happens that the local no-good cowboy Billy Drake is caught cheating, and he is riddled with bullets by one of his fellow participants. These are no-good, dirty cowboys, but they still have manners, and seeing as Drake was married, they agree that someone should notify his wife that her no-good husband is dead.

Of course, this is not a chore that any of the cowboys want to undertake, so they decide the stalemate the best way they know how—by drawing cards. The one who pulls the lowest card has to go tell her.

The losing cowboy reluctantly wanders over to the widow's shack and knocks on the door. A big, surly-looking woman answers the door.

With his hat in his hand, the cowboy asks, "Are you the Widow Drake?"

"Widder? I ain't no widder."

"Ma'am," the cowboy says, holding up a playing card, "this here three of spades says you is!"

Slow-hand Poetry

When men lived raw in the desert's maw,
And Hell was nothing to shun.
Where they buried 'em neat
Without a preacher or sheet,

And writ on their headboards
Crude but sweet,
"This jasper was slow with a gun."
—author unknown

This Just In!

Two cowboy outlaws escape from a jail in Winnipeg. One is eight-feet tall and the other is four-feet tall. The sheriff and his posse of men search for them high and low.

The Lone, Lone Ranger

The Lone Ranger and Tonto are riding through the plains when suddenly they are surrounded by thousands of Indian warriors.

"It looks like this will be the end of our journey together, friend," the Lone Ranger says to Tonto sadly.

Walking away slowly, Tonto says, "What do you mean, paleface?"

Is that a Fact?

It is illegal to tie a horse in front of city hall in Yukon, Oklahoma. In the state, it is also illegal to wear your boots to bed. Now that's just silly!

It is illegal in the county of Carrizozo, New Mexico, for any woman to appear unshaven in public. Thank heavens for that, but what kind of women live in Carrizozo?

True Story

A long time ago in the town of Eureka, Nevada, a handsome cowboy waltzes into town. He is tall, well built, blue-eyed and has the most manly mustache anyone has ever seen. All the ladies swoon over him when he rides through town, but only one woman catches his eye—the mayor's beautiful daughter.

Q: What did the cowboy maggot say when he went into the saloon bar?

A: Gimme a slug of whiskey.

The mayor does not like cowboys and does not like this cowboy stranger making advances on his daughter. But his daughter falls in love with the cowboy, and as children always do, she disobeys her father and runs off with the handsome mustachioed cowboy. The mayor is so upset that he makes a new law that exists to this day. He forbade any men with mustaches from kissing women.

Blonde Cowgirl on Death Row

Three cowgirls are about to be executed for their crimes. One of them is a brunette, one's a redhead and one's a blonde.

Two guards bring the brunette forward, and the executioner asks if she has any last requests. She says no, and the executioner shouts, "Ready!...Aim!..."

Suddenly, the brunette yells, "Earthquake!" Everyone is startled and looks around. She manages to escape.

The angry guards then bring the redhead forward, and the executioner asks if she has any last requests. She says no, and the executioner shouts, "Ready!... Aim!..."

The redhead then screams, "Tornado!" Yet again, everyone is startled and looks around. She too escapes execution.

By this point, the blonde cowgirl has figured out what the other cowgirls did. The guards bring her forward, and the executioner asks if she has any last requests. She also says no, and the executioner shouts, "Ready!...Aim!..."

The blonde cowgirl shouts, "Fire!"

Old-timer Justice

An old prospector leading a tired old mule shuffles into a small town in Oregon. He heads straight for the only saloon in town to clear his parched throat. He walks up to the saloon and ties his old mule to the hitching post.

As he stands there brushing the trail dust from his face and clothes, a young gunslinger steps out of the saloon with a gun in one hand and a bottle of whiskey in the other.

The young gunslinger looks at the old man, laughs, and says, "Hey, old man, can you dance?"

The old man looks up at the gunslinger and says, "No, son, I don't dance—never really wanted to."

A crowd has gathered as the gunslinger grins and says, "Well, you old fool, you're gonna dance now!" and he starts shooting at the old man's feet.

The old prospector, not wanting to get a toe blown off, hops around like a flea on a hot skillet. Everybody standing around starts to laugh.

When he fires his last bullet, the young gunslinger, still laughing, holsters his gun and turns around to go back into the saloon.

The old man turns to his pack mule, pulls out a double-barreled 12-gauge shotgun and cocks both hammers. The loud clicks carry clearly through the air. The crowd stops laughing immediately.

The young gunslinger hears the sounds too, and he turns around very slowly. The silence is deafening. The crowd watches as the young gunman stares at the old-timer and the large gaping holes of the shotgun barrels.

The shotgun never wavers in the old man's hands as he quietly says, "Son, have you ever kissed a mule's ass?"

The gunslinger swallows hard and says, "No, sir—but I've always wanted to."

Cheatin'!

Four cowboys are at an old saloon in Tombstone playing poker. A lot of money is at stake, and each cowboy is keeping a sharp eye on the other.

As one of the players calls the hand and lays down his cards, another player stands up in amazement and says, "Hey! George is cheatin'! He ain't playin' the cards I dealt him!"

Cowboy Wisdom
Whiskey—the reason I wake up every afternoon.

Lord, Save Me!

One day in a small town in Manitoba during really stormy weather, a flood occurs. Everyone rushes to lifeboats and begins to flee. But in a church, a devout cowboy sits on the altar and does not move.

A man runs up to him and says, "Come quickly! We have a lifeboat ready for you."

The cowboy replies, "No. There is no need for me to flee because the Lord will provide, and he will save me."

"Suit yourself," says the man.

A few hours later, the water rises up to the altar where the cowboy is sitting. A lifeboat zooms through the door with a few men in it.

One man calls to the cowboy, "Come quickly!"

The cowboy says, "No, for the Lord will provide, and he will save me."

So the lifeboat zooms off. A few hours later, the water rises up to the crucifix on the wall on which the cowboy is hanging. Another lifeboat zooms into the church.

The man in the boat says to the cowboy, "The town is flooding. You must come with us to safety."

"No. The Lord will provide. He will save me," says the cowboy.

Many hours later, the water rises up to the roof of the church, and the cowboy drowns. Later, in heaven, the cowboy meets God and says, "Lord, why didn't you save me? I had so much faith that you would provide."

God says, "What are you talking about! I sent you three bloody lifeboats!"

Solitary

Three outlaws are sentenced to 25 years of solitary confinement for robbing a local bank. As a gesture of goodwill before locking up the outlaws, the prison warden allows each prisoner to take one item into his cell. The first outlaw asks for a pile of books, the second asks for his wife and the third asks for 200 cartons of cigarettes.

> **Q:** Who's the most alcoholic cowboy in the Wild West?
>
> **A:** John Wine.

At the end of the 25-year sentence, the prisoners are released. The first prisoner says, "Those books saved my life. I've studied so hard that now I will become a lawyer."

The second prisoner steps out of his cell with his wife and five new children and says, "My wife and

I have never been so close. I have a beautiful new family, and I am really happy."

When the third guy leaves his cell, he says, "Anyone got a match?"

Funeral Story

In the Wild West, things were done a little differently. To illustrate the point, I will tell you about the experience of a widow at her cowboy husband's funeral.

Minutes before her husband's funeral, this widow decides to take one last look at his body.

To her horror, she sees that he is wearing a brown suit whereas she issued strict orders to the undertaker that she wants him buried in a blue suit.

> **Cowboy Wisdom**
> *It is easier to get an actor to be a cowboy than to get a cowboy to be an actor.*

She finds the undertaker and demands that the suit be changed. At first, the undertaker tries to tell her it is too late, but when he sees the anger and sadness on her face, he orders the mortician to wheel the coffin away.

A few minutes later, just as the funeral is about to start, the coffin is wheeled back in and incredibly, the woman's husband is now wearing a blue suit. The widow is delighted, and after the service, she praises the undertaker for his swift work.

"'Twas nothin', ma'am," he says. "It just so happened there was another body in the back room, and he was already dressed in a blue suit. All we had to do was switch the heads."

Grandpappy

Two cowboys are bragging about their families when one says, "My grandpappy predicted the year that he would die. What's more, he knew the exact month he was going to die, the precise day he was going to die and even the time he was going to die. And he was right on every count."

"That's uncanny!" says his friend. "How did he know?"

"The judge told him."

Cannibals

A Frenchman, an Englishman and a cowboy are captured by a cannibal tribe. The chief tells the men, "You will each be killed, then you will be skinned and we will use your skin to build a canoe, and finally, we will cook and eat your organs. As a concession, I will allow you to choose how you want to die."

Q: Why did the cowboy ride his horse?

A: Because the horse was too heavy to carry.

The Frenchman asks for a sword and yells, "Vive la France!" and runs the sword through his chest.

The Englishman asks for a gun and yells, "God Save the Queen!" and blows his brains out.

The cowboy says, "Gimme a fork!" and immediately starts jabbing himself all over his body until blood is pouring through hundreds of holes.

"What on earth are you doing?" asks the chief.

The cowboy last words: "There goes yer goddamn canoe!"

Genie

Three businessmen—a New Yorker, a Californian and a Texan—attend a conference in Seattle and are out walking after lunch when they come across a lantern. As they examine it, a genie pops out and declares, "I will give you each one wish for freeing me from my prison."

The New Yorker says, "I work on Wall Street, and I want you to make all my investments generate millions of dollars so I can one day be rich enough to become governor of New York." There is a puff of smoke, and the genie says the wish has been granted.

Next, it is the Californian's turn. "I want a wall around California so that no foreigners can come into our precious state," he says. There is again a puff of smoke, and the genie grants his wish.

Finally, it is the Texan's turn. "Tell me about this wall around California," he says to the genie.

"Well," replies the genie, "the wall is about 150 feet high, 50 feet thick and completely surrounds the state. No one can get in or out."

"Interesting," says the Texan. "Fill it with water!"

Water!

A cowboy lost in the Nevada desert is desperate for water when he sees something in the distance. Hoping it's water, he hurries toward the image, only to find that it is an old Indian man selling neckties at a small stand.

The cowboy asks, "Do you have water?"

The Indian man replies, "I have no water. But would you like to buy a tie? They are only $5 each."

The cowboy shouts, "I don't need an overpriced tie! I need water! I should kill you, but I must find water first!"

"Okay, okay," says the old Indian man. "It does not matter that you do not want to buy a tie and that you hate me. I will show you that I am bigger man than that. If you continue over that hill to the east for about two miles, you will find a lovely restaurant. It has all the ice-cold water you need. Good luck."

Muttering to himself, the cowboy staggers away over the hill. Several hours later, almost dead, he staggers back to the old Indian and says, "Your damn brother won't let me in without a damn tie!"

I Fought the Law and I Won

Q: What do you call a dinosaur wearing a cowboy hat?

A: Tyrannosaurus Tex.

Cowboy (after being sentenced to 90 days in jail for cattle rustling): "May I address the court?"

Judge: "Of course."

Cowboy: "If I called you a son of a bitch, what would you do?"

Judge: "I'd hold you in contempt and assess an additional five days in jail."

Cowboy: "What if I thought you were a son of a bitch?"

Judge: "I can't do anything about that. There's no law against thinking."

Cowboy: "In that case, I think you're a son of a bitch."

Mourning

A man goes into a bar one day and sees a friend at a table, drinking by himself.

Approaching the cowboy, the man says, "You look terrible. What's the problem?"

"My momma died in June," he says, "and left me $10,000."

"Gee, that's tough," the man replies.

"Then in July," the cowboy continues, "my pappy died, leavin' me $50,000."

"Wow. Two parents gone in two months. No wonder you're depressed."

"And last month, my old aunt died and left me her ranch."

"Three close family members lost in three months? How sad."

"Then this month," continues the friend, "nothing!"

Job Description

Three cowboys in the Old West are traveling through Indian country on horseback. One day, they stumble onto a tent filled with 100 beautiful women. The men start getting friendly with all the women, when suddenly an old man enters the tent.

> **Cowboy Wisdom**
> Treat a woman like a racehorse, and she'll never be a nag.

"I am the chief, and I am the master of all these women," says the old man. "No one else can touch them except me. You must pay for what you have done today. You will be punished in a way corresponding to your profession."

The chief turns to the first man and asks him what he does for a living.

"I'm a sheriff," says the first man.

"Then we will shoot your penis off!" says the chief.

The chief then turns to the second man and asks him what he does for a living.

"I'm a logger," says the second man.

"Then we will chop your penis off!" says the chief.

Finally, the chief asks the last man, "And you, what do you do for a living?"

And the third cowboy answers, "I'm a lollipop salesman!"

Smiling Faces, Deadly Places

Three bodies turn up at the local undertaker's, all with huge smiles on their faces. The undertaker calls in the sheriff to report the causes of death.

"First body: City boy. Died smiling, of heart failure while making love to his mistress. Second body: Rancher. Won $1000 gambling. Spent it all on whiskey. Died smiling, of alcohol poisoning. Third body: Cowboy. Died smiling after being struck by lightning."

"Why was the last cowboy smiling?" asks the sheriff.

The undertaker replies, "He thought he was having his picture taken."

In Hell

One day, a mean old cowboy dies and finds himself in hell. As he is wallowing in despair, he has his first meeting with the devil.

Devil: "Why so glum, chum?"

Cowboy: "What do you think? I'm in hell!"

Devil: "Hell's not so bad. We actually have a lot of fun down here. You a drinkin' man?"

Cowboy: "Sure, I love to drink."

Devil: "Well, you're gonna love Mondays then. On Mondays, all we do is drink. Whiskey, tequila,

Guinness, vodka, rum. We drink till we throw up, and then we drink some more."

Cowboy: "Gee, that sounds great!"

Devil: "You a smoker?"

Cowboy: "You better believe it!"

Devil: "Alright! You're gonna love Tuesdays. We get the finest cigars from all over the world, and we smoke our lungs out. If you get cancer, no biggie—you're already dead."

Cowboy: "Wow. That's awesome!"

Devil: "I bet you like to gamble."

Cowboy: "Why, yes, as a matter of fact I do."

> **Q:** What did the buffalo say to his offspring while running away from a cowboy trying to hunt him?
>
> **A:** Bison!

Devil: "Good, because on Wednesdays you can gamble all you want. Craps, blackjack, roulette, poker, slots, whatever. If you go bankrupt, well, you're dead anyhow."

Cowboy: "Sounds good to me!"

Devil: "You into drugs?"

Cowboy: "Are you kiddin'? I love drugs. You don't mean…"

Devil: "That's right. Thursday is drug day. Help yourself to a great big bowl of crack or smack. Smoke a doobie the size of a submarine. You can do all the drugs you want, and if ya overdose, who cares? You're dead!"

Cowboy: "Yowza! I never realized hell was such a swingin' place."

Devil: "You one of them Brokeback cowboys?"

Cowboy: "No…"

Devil (grimaces): "Oh…you're gonna hate Fridays."

Heaven Bound

Father Murphy walks into a saloon and says to the first cowboy he sees, "Do you want to go to heaven?"

"I do, Father," replies the cowboy

The priest says, "Leave this pub right now!" He then approaches a second cowboy and says, "Do you want to go to heaven?"

"Certainly, Father," is the man's reply.

"Then leave this den of Satan!" orders the priest.

Father Murphy then walks up to Cowboy Wyatt and asks, "Do you want to go to heaven?"

Wyatt replies, "No, I don't, Father."

The priest looks him right in the eye and says, "You mean to tell me that when you die you don't want to go to heaven?"

Wyatt smiles and says, "Oh, when I die, yes, Father. I thought you were getting a group together to go right now."

Death Row

Three convicts are on a bus on their way to prison. They are each allowed to take one item with them to help them occupy their time while incarcerated.

On the bus, one turns to another and says, "So, what did you bring?"

The second convict pulls out a box of paints and states that he intends to paint anything he can. He says he wants to become the "Grandma Moses of Jail."

Then he asks the first convict, "What did you bring?"

The first convict pulls out a deck of cards and grins. "I brought cards. I can play poker, solitaire, gin and any number of card games."

The third convict, who just happens to be a cowboy, is sitting quietly aside, grinning to himself. The other two take notice, and one of them asks, "Why are you so smug? What did you bring?"

The cowboy pulls out a box of tampons and smiles. He says, "I brought these."

The other two are puzzled, and one of them asks, "What can you do with those?"

The cowboy grins, points to the box and says, "Well, according to the box, I can go horseback riding, swimming, roller-skating…"

Could Be Worse

Two deputies—one who has been in the town for 10 years and the other who has just transferred—answer an emergency call. When they walk into the house, they find the nude bodies of a man and a woman in the bedroom. They have been shot to death. When the deputies go to the living room, they find the body of a man with a gun at his side.

Q: What advice do cows give?

A: Turn the udder cheek and mooooove on!

"No doubt about it," the new deputy says, "this was a double murder and suicide. This guy came home, found his wife in bed with somebody else and shot them both. Then he shot himself."

"You're right," the experienced deputy replies. "But I'll bet you $50 when the sheriff gets here, he's going to say, 'It could have been worse.'"

"No way. You're on."

The old sheriff arrives at the scene. "No doubt about it," he says, shaking his head. "It was a double murder and suicide." After hesitating for a moment, the sheriff looks his deputies in the eyes. "But, you know," he says, "it could have been worse."

The new deputy who has lost the bet, jumps up and shouts, "Sheriff, how could it have been worse?! There are three dead people in this house. It couldn't have been worse."

"Yes, it could," the sheriff retorts. "You see that guy there on the floor? If the husband had come home yesterday, that would be me!"

Evil

Q: Why do cowsirls walk bow-legged?

A: Because cowboys eat with their hats on.

Two mean brothers live in a small Old West Texas town. They are rich and use their money to keep their evil ways from the public eye. They even attend church and look to be perfect Christians.

Then, the pastor from their church retires, and a new one is hired. Not only can the new priest see right through the brothers' deception, but he also speaks well and true, which brings more people to church. A fund-raising campaign is started to build a new assembly hall to fit all the new parishioners.

All of a sudden, one of the brothers dies. The remaining brother seeks out the new pastor the day before the funeral and hands him a check for the amount needed to finish paying for the new church.

"I have only one condition," the man says to the priest. "At my brother's funeral, you must say my brother was a saint." The pastor gives his word and deposits the check.

At the funeral, the pastor does not hold back. "He was an evil man," he says. "He cheated on his wife and abused his family." After going on in this vein for a short time, he concludes his sermon with, "But, compared to his brother, he was a saint."

CHAPTER SEVEN

Modern vs. Old-time Cowboys

Church Goer

Cowboy Joe is telling his fellow cowboys back on the ranch about his first visit to a big-city church.

"When I got there, they had me park my old truck in the corral," says Joe.

"You mean the *parking lot*," interrupts Charlie, a more worldly fellow.

"I walked up the trail to the door," Joe continues.

"The *sidewalk* to the door," says Charlie, correcting him.

"Inside the door, I was met by this dude," Joe goes on.

"That would be the *usher*," Charlie explains.

"Well, the usher led me down the chute," Joe says.

"You mean the *aisle*," says Charlie.

"Then he led me to a stall and told me to sit there," Joe continued.

"*Pew*," Charlie retorts.

"Yeah," says Joe. "That's what that pretty lady said when I sat down beside her."

Newbie Cowboy

A city slicker buys a ranch out west where he intends to raise cattle. A friend comes to visit and asks if the ranch has a name.

"Well," says the wanna-be cowboy. "I wanted to call it the 'Bar-J,' but my wife favored the name 'Suzy-Q,' one son liked the 'Flying-W' and the other son wanted the 'Lazy-Y.' So, we're calling it the 'Bar-J-Suzy-Q-Flying-W-Lazy-Y.'"

"But where are all your cattle?" asks his friend.

"None have survived the branding."

Curious Kid

A kid walks up to a guy wearing a 10-gallon hat, leather vest, chaps and sneakers. The kid asks him, "Mr. Cowboy, why do you wear that big hat?"

> **Cowboy Wisdom**
> Behind every successful rancher is a wife who works in town.

The cowboy replies, "Well, son, this big ol' hat protects me from the hot sun 'n' drivin' rain, and at night, I puts it over muh face when I sleeps on the range, so it protects me then, too."

"Why do you wear that leather vest, Mr. Cowboy?"

"The vest? Why, it also helps to keep the weather offa me, and it has nice pockets where I stashes muh valuables."

"Well, why do you wear leather chaps?"

"They protect muh legs when I'm drivin' this here horse through mesquite 'n' cactus."

"Say, Mr. Cowboy," the kid finally asks, "why do you wear those sneakers?"

"That's so's nobody'll think I'm some damned truck driver!"

Visitor

One day a New Yorker stops in the small southern Alberta town of Pincher Creek. When he gets out of his car, the wind is blowing so hard that he has to lean into the wind as he walks to keep it from blowing him down.

As he approaches a street corner, he spots a cowboy standing there holding onto the lamp post. He asks the man, "Does the wind blow like this all the time?"

Q: Why did the cowboy push his wife off the cliff?

A: Tequila!

"No, sir," is the reply. "Sometimes it changes and comes from the other direction."

Nobs!

A wife and her husband go horseback riding at a dude ranch in Nevada for the first time. The cowboy preparing the horses asks the woman if she wants a Western or English saddle. The woman asks the cowboy what the difference is.

He tells her that one has a horn and the other one doesn't.

The woman says, "The one without the horn is fine. I don't expect we'll run into too much traffic."

Discussion

A young, well-educated man on a business trip gets on the plane to find himself seated next to an older, weathered man wearing a Western snap shirt, faded jeans and a cowboy hat. Thinking himself above the old cowboy, the young man decides to make sport of him.

"You know," he says, "I've heard these flights go more quickly if you strike up a conversation with a fellow passenger. So, let's talk."

The cowboy looks at him wryly and says, "Well, I s'pose that'd be all right. What would ya like to discuss?"

"Oh, I don't know," says the young man with a hint of sarcasm. "How about nuclear proliferation?"

"Hmmm," says the cowboy, sensing the man's attempt to belittle him. "That could be an interesting topic. But let me ask ya one question first. Horses, cows and deer all eat the same stuff—grass. Yet, a deer passes little pellets, a cow turns out a flat patty and a horse makes muffins of dried poop. Why do you s'pose that is?"

Dumbfounded, the young man replies, "I haven't the slightest idea."

"So tell me then," says the cowboy with a smile. "How is it that ya feel qualified to discuss nukes when you don't know shit?"

President's Men

A city slicker walks into a cowboy bar and orders a beer just as former President Bush appears on the TV above the bar. After a few sips, the stranger looks up at the television and mumbles, "Now, there's the biggest horse's ass I've ever seen."

> **Cowboy Wisdom**
> If it doesn't seem to be worth the effort, it probably ain't.

A customer at the end of the bar quickly stands up, walks over to the stranger and decks him.

A few minutes later, as the man is finishing his beer, Mrs. Bush appears on the television. "She's a horse's ass too," says the man.

This time, a cowboy sitting at the other end of the bar stands up, walks over to the stranger and knocks him off his stool.

"Damn it!" says the man, climbing back up onto his stool. "This must be Bush country!"

"Nope," replies the bartender. "Horse country."

At the Movies

Two fellas are watching an old Western movie, and it comes to the part when a cowboy on his horse heads at full gallop right toward a cliff.

One of the guys says to the other, "Hey, I'll bet you $10 that he rides over the cliff."

The other guy says, "You're on!"

Well, the cowboy and the horse in the movie go right over the cliff. The fella that lost the bet pays up. A while later, the guy who won says, "Hey, I'm feeling a little guilty about our bet and need to make a confession—I already saw the movie."

The other fella replies, "Well, I also seen the movie before, but I didn't think he'd do it again!"

Cowboy and the Government

A cowboy has spent many days crossing the Texas plains without water. His horse has already died of thirst. The cowboy is crawling through the sand, certain that he has taken his last breath, when all of a sudden he sees an object sticking out of the sand several yards ahead of him. He crawls to the object, pulls it out of the sand and discovers what looks to be an old briefcase. The cowboy opens it, and out pops a genie.

Cowboy Wisdom
There are two theories to arguin' with a woman. Neither one works.

But this is no ordinary genie. It is a woman, and she is wearing a dull gray dress with a government ID badge pinned to her chest. There's a calculator in her hand, and she has a pencil tucked behind one ear.

Q: Why was the cowboy a lot of laughs?

A: He was always horsing around.

"Well, cowboy," says the genie. "You know how I work. You have three wishes."

"I'm not falling for this," says the cowboy. "I'm not going to trust a government genie."

"What do you have to lose? You have no transportation and no water, and it looks like you're a goner anyway!"

The cowboy thinks about this for a minute and decides that the genie is right.

"Okay. I wish I was in a lush oasis with plenty of food and drink."

POOF!

The cowboy finds himself in the most beautiful oasis he has ever seen, and he is surrounded with jugs of beer and platters of delicacies.

"Okay, cowpoke, what's your second wish?" asks the genie.

"My second wish is that I was rich beyond my wildest dreams."

POOF!

The cowboy is surrounded by treasure chests filled with rare gold coins and precious gems.

"Okay, cowpuncher, you have just one more wish. Better make it a good one!" says the genie.

After thinking for a few minutes, the cowboy says, "I wish that no matter where I go, beautiful women will want and need me."

POOF!

The cowboy is turned into a tampon.

The moral of the story: If the government offers you anything, there's going to be a string attached!

Young Buck

Little Johnny loves to pretend he is a cowboy. He lives and breathes everything to do with the Old West. He always dresses up like a cowboy and tries his best to talk like a cowboy.

One day, while Johnny's dad is mowing the lawn in the backyard, and his mom is inside the house, Johnny is playing Cowboys and Indians in the front yard.

Suddenly, Johnny comes sprinting into the backyard and points to smoke coming out of their house and screams, "Dad! Look! Mom must be signaling us that dinner is ready!"

> **Cowboy Wisdom**
> Never kick a fresh turd on a hot day.

Heard on an Airplane

A Baptist preacher is seated next to a cowboy on a flight to Montana.

After the plane takes off, the cowboy asks for a whiskey and soda, which the flight attendant brings to him.

The flight attendant then asks the preacher if he would like a drink. Appalled, the preacher replies, "I'd rather be tied up and taken advantaged of by women of ill-repute than to let liquor touch my lips."

The cowboy then hands his drink back to the flight attendant and says, "Me, too. I didn't know we had a choice."

Old Traditions

Three cowboys are at the open-casket funeral of their dear friend.

The first one says, "There's a legend in my family that if you bury a man with a little bit of money, it will help him in the afterlife," and he reaches into his pocket, pulls out $10 and puts it in the casket.

The second cowboy wasn't planning on it, but he pulls out $10 from his wallet and lays it in the casket.

The third cowboy has a reputation for being cheap, so he looks at the first two and says, "What? You think I won't put in too? I'll put in $20!"

Then he writes a check for $40, drops it in the casket and takes the two $10 bills as change.

Dreamer

A little boy walks into a pet shop and asks the clerk if the store sells dachshunds. The clerk says yes, and she goes to the back and returns with the dog and hands it to the boy.

The boy is all excited when he holds the dog and immediately gives the clerk a check for $100, which he says was his birthday money. The clerk asks him why he wants that dog so much and not a big dog like most boys get when they come into the store.

> Did you know that cowboys in a rodeo can be sure to get a few bucks?

He replies, "I've always wanted to be a cowboy, and now I can because the song says 'Get along little doggie!'"

Too Relaxed

A cowboy lays sprawled across three entire seats in a posh Amarillo movie theater. When the usher walks by and notices, he whispers to the cowboy, "Sorry, sir, but you're only allowed one seat."

The cowboy groans but doesn't budge.

The usher becomes more impatient. "Sir, if you don't get up from there, I'm going to have to call the manager."

The cowboy just groans again.

The usher marches briskly back up the aisle to the door. In a moment, he returns with the manager. Together, the two of them repeatedly tell the cowboy to move, but with no success. Finally, they summon the police.

The cop who arrives surveys the situation briefly then asks the cowboy, "All right, buddy, what's your name?"

"Sam," the cowboy moans.

"Where ya from, Sam?"

With pain in his voice, Sam replies, "The balcony."

Wise Natives

It is October, and the Indians on a remote reservation in North Dakota ask their new chief if the coming winter is going to be cold or mild.

Since he is a chief in a modern society, he has never been taught the old secrets to predict weather.

When he looks at the sky, he can't tell what the winter is going to be like.

Nevertheless, to be on the safe side, he tells his tribe that the winter is indeed going to be cold and that the members of the village should collect firewood to be prepared.

But being a practical leader, after several days he gets an idea. He calls the National Weather Service and asks, "Is the coming winter going to be cold?"

"It looks like this winter is going to be quite cold," the meteorologist at the weather service responds.

So the chief goes back to his people and tells them to collect even more firewood in order to be prepared.

A week later, the chief calls the National Weather Service again. "Does it still look like it is going to be a very cold winter?" the chief asks.

"Yes," the man at National Weather Service again replies, "it's going to be a very cold winter."

The chief goes back to his people again and orders them to collect every scrap of firewood they can find.

Two weeks later, the chief calls the National Weather Service again. "Are you absolutely sure that the winter is going to be very cold?"

"Absolutely," the man replies. "It's looking more and more like it's going to be one of the coldest winters ever."

"How can you be so sure?" the chief asks.

The weatherman replies, "We're sure it's going to be cold because the Indians are collecting firewood like crazy!"

Big City Hotel

A Tennessee cowboy has long heard tales about the big city, so finally he ventures out east and rambles into New York City. Not knowing anyone, he checks into a big city hotel and is shocked when they charge him $200 for his room. He finally concedes to pay the outlandish price, but when the porter tries to lead him into the hotel's elevator, the old cowboy stops dead in his tracks.

"No sir!" the cowboy screams. "I ain't gonna pay $200 for no little dinky such as that!"

Mirror, Mirror

After living in the remote wilderness of Texas all his life, an old cowboy decides it's time to visit the big city of Austin. In one of the stores, he picks up a mirror and looks in it. Not ever having seen a mirror before, he remarks at the image staring back at him, "How about that! Here's a picture of my daddy."

Q: What did the horse say when it fell?

A: I've fallen, and I can't giddy-up!

He buys the mirror, thinking it is a picture of his daddy who passed on years ago, but on the way home, he remembers that his wife didn't like his father. So he hangs the mirror up in the barn, and every morning, he goes there and looks at it.

His wife begins to get suspicious of her husband's many trips to the barn. One day, after her husband leaves to run errands, she searches the barn and finds the mirror. As she looks into the glass, she fumes, "So that's the ugly bitch he's runnin' around with."

Texans' Ingenuity

After digging to a depth of 10 yards, New York scientists find traces of copper wire dating back 100 years and conclude that their ancestors already had a telephone network more than 100 years ago.

Not to be outdone by the New Yorkers, California scientists dig to a depth of 20 yards, and shortly after, an article in the *LA Times* newspaper states: "California archaeologists find traces of 200-year-old copper wire and have concluded that their ancestors already had an advanced high-tech communications network 100 years earlier than the New Yorkers."

If you wear a coonskin cap with a tail on it, does that make you a butt-head?

One week later, *The Express News,* a local newspaper in Texas reports the following: "After digging as deep as 30 yards in corn fields near College Station, Texas A&M University, Bubba Johnson, a self-taught archaeologist, reports that he found absolutely nothing. Bubba therefore concludes that 300 years ago, Texas had already gone wireless!

Wanna Go Hunting?

While in hospital, Mike the cowboy is explaining to the sheriff why his cousin shot him.

"Well," Mike begins, "we was havin' a good time drinkin' and all, when my cousin Hank picked up his shotgun and says, 'Hey, do you fellas wanna go hunting?'"

"Then what happened?" asks the sheriff.

"From what I remember," replies Mike, "I stood up and hollered, 'Sure, I'm game!'"

911

Emily Sue and her husband Jake Steed live out in the middle of the Montana mountains. When Emily Sue passes away one day, Jake calls 911.

The 911 operator tells Jake that she will send someone out right away. "Where do you live?" asks the operator.

Jake replies, "At the end of Eucalyptus Drive."

The operator asked, "Can you spell that for me?"

After a long pause, Jake finally says, "How 'bout I drag her over to Oak Street and you pick her up there? Would take me less time than spelling my street."

Cowboy Wisdom
The only good reason to ride a bull is to meet a nurse.

Clever Cowboy

A Colorado state trooper pulls over a cowboy driving a pickup truck on I-40. The state trooper says to the driver, "Got any ID?"

The cowboy says, "'Bout what?"

Idiot Fishing

Two cowboys are taking a break from their ranching duties to fish out in the local lake.

The first guy reels in his line and sees he has snagged a bottle. As he's taking it off the hook, a genie pops out and offers him one wish.

"Turn the lake into beer!" he says.

The genie says, "Poof!" and the lake turns to beer.

He says to his friend, "Hey, buddy, look! I turned the lake into beer. How's 'bout that?"

The other guy says, "You idiot! Now we have to piss in the boat!"

Phone Call

The phone at Old Man John's Texas ranch rings one evening.

When he answers, the operator says, "This is long distance from Chicago."

"Ah knowed it's a long distance from Chicago!" answers the cowboy. "How come ya called to tell me that?"

Politicians

A bus load of politicians is speeding along a country road when the bus crashes into a tree and overturns. There is blood and glass everywhere. An old cowboy living next to the road sees the crash and is the first on the scene. Within two hours, he digs a big hole and buries all the politicians.

A few days later, the local sheriff is passing through the area when he sees the wreckage of the bus. He goes to the nearest house and asks the old cowboy who answers the door if he saw what happened. The cowboy says he did.

"Were the occupants all dead?" asks the sheriff.

"Well," says the old cowboy. "Some of them said they weren't, but you know how dem politicians lie."

Feminist

A radical feminist gets on a bus traveling through cow country when a cowboy sitting in the front of the bus gets up from his seat. The woman thinks to herself, *Here's another one of them gallant cowboys patronizing the female sex by offering a poor woman his seat.* She pushes him back down into his seat without saying a word.

A few minutes later, the man again tries to get up but again the woman pushes him back down. Finally, the cowboy says, "Look, ma'am, you've got to let me up. I'm already a mile past my stop."

New Parenting

Four friends are sitting together in a bar when one gets up to go to the bathroom. While he's gone, the three other guys start to talk about their sons.

The first says, "Mine was a big worry for me. I did not think he was ever going to make something of himself, but he is doing okay now. He owns a car dealership and even bought his friend a new car."

The second says, "Mine was hopeless in school. He had failure written all over him. I was sure he would become a criminal. But he pulled through. He now manages a bank and just gave his best friend a $1 million savings bond."

The third says, "My son was bad at school too, but I'm glad to announce that now he is fine. He owns a pet shop, and just gave his best friend a puppy."

Just then the fourth guy returns. "We were talking about ours sons," says one of the men at the table.

"Oh, mine was a real headache," says the fourth guy, who happened to be a cowboy from Alberta. "He's gay. At first I had a huge problem with that, me being a good Christian, but he is my son, and after all, Jesus teaches us to love everyone. My son is actually doing fine in the world. Just recently, one of his boyfriends gave him a new car, another gave him a million dollars and another gave him a puppy. So I couldn't be more proud."

Railroads

A country boy gets off a train after a long trip. His face is as white as a sheet. A friend picking him up from the station asks him what is wrong.

"Railroad sickness," says the country boy. "Whenever I travel by train, I always feel sick if I sit with my back to the engine."

"Why didn't you ask the person sitting opposite you to change places?" asks his friend.

"I thought of that," replies the country boy, "but there wasn't anybody there."

Religious Cowboy

An old cowboy preacher has a teenage son, and it was getting time the boy should give some thought to choosing a profession. Like many young men, the boy doesn't really know what he wants to do, and he doesn't seem too concerned about it.

> Knock, knock!
> Who's there?
> Little old lady.
> Little old lady who?
> Hey, I didn't know you could yodel!

One day, while the boy is away at school, his father decides to try an experiment. He goes into the boy's bedroom and places three objects on the bedside table: a Bible, a silver dollar and a bottle of whiskey.

"I'll just hide behind the door," the old preacher says to himself, "and when he comes home from school this afternoon, I'll see which object he picks up. If it's the Bible, he's going to be a preacher like me, and what a blessing that would be! If he picks up the dollar, he's going to be a businessman, and that would be okay, too.

But if he picks up the bottle, he's going to be a no-good drunkard, and, Lord, what a shame that would be."

The old man waits anxiously and soon hears his son's footsteps as he enters the house and heads for his room. He tosses his books on the bed, and as he turns to leave the room, he spots the objects on the table. With curiosity in his eye, he walks over to inspect them. He picks up the Bible and places it under his arm, drops the silver dollar into his pocket, uncorks the bottle and takes a swig.

"Oh, lord," the old man whispers, "he's gonna be a congressman!"

Magic

A cowboy and his family are visiting the big city of Houston, Texas, for the first time, and they stay at hotel. The father and son are in the hotel lobby when they spot an elevator.

"What's that, Pa?" the boy asks.

"I never saw nothin' like that in my life," says the father.

Seconds later, an old frail woman walks into the hotel and hobbles to the elevator. She presses the button with her cane, waits for the doors to open and gets in.

The father and son, still amazed by this contraption, continue to watch.

They hear a ping noise, and the elevator doors open again. Out steps a beautiful 20-year-old busty blonde woman.

The father looks at his son and says, "Go get your mother!"

Top Ten Modern Cowboy Towns

1. Deadwood, South Dakota
2. Miles City, Montana
3. Sheridan, Wyoming
4. Dodge City, Kansas
5. Calgary, Alberta
6. Elko, Nevada
7. Tombstone, Arizona
8. White Oaks, New Mexico
9. Bandera, Texas
10. Oklahoma City, Oklahoma

City Boys

A city slicker named Tommy is on vacation in Wyoming. His hosts, being very hospitable, take him to the local rodeo, especially to see the greatest bucking bronco of all time, Blue Steel.

Blue Steel is famed and renowned throughout the West for being the toughest, meanest horse there ever was. The horse has bucked off so many riders that the rodeo organizers promise $10,000 to anyone who can ride him just for 10 seconds.

All the local cowboys try their best to ride the horse, but Blue Steel lives up to his reputation and throws them all off with the greatest of ease.

As a joke, the organizers then offer the prize to anyone in the crowd who would dare to tangle with such a beast.

Up jumps Tommy, and of course, everyone laughs at him. But the organizers decide to let the city boy have a try.

Blue Steel bucks and lunges, but Tommy not only stays on the horse for 10 seconds, he stays on for 20 seconds, then 30, then a full minute! After a few minutes more, Blue Steel is so exhausted that he calms down, and Tommy rides him all around the arena like the horse is a birthday party pony.

Everyone is astonished.

"Considering you've never even sat on a horse before," says Tommy's friends, "how on earth did you manage that?"

"Easy," says Tommy, "my wife's an epileptic."

Hearing Aid

A retired cowboy says to his neighbor, "After a life on the ranch, screaming at bulls and operating heavy machines, I went deaf so I just bought a new hearing aid. It cost me $4000, but it's state-of-the-art. It's perfect."

"Really?" says the neighbor. "What kind is it?"

"Twelve thirty."

Mail

A man is in his front yard mowing grass when his attractive cowgirl neighbor comes out of her house and goes straight to her mailbox. She opens it, then slams it shut and storms back into the house.

A little later, the blonde cowgirl comes out of her house again, goes to the mailbox and opens it and slams it shut. Angrily, back into the house she goes.

As the man is getting ready to edge his lawn, she comes out of her house again, marches to the mailbox, opens it and then slams it closed, harder than ever.

Puzzled by the woman's actions, the man asks her, "Is something wrong?"

The cowgirl replies, "There certainly is! My stupid computer keeps saying, 'You've Got Mail.'"

Western Technology

A New Yorker, a Californian and a cowboy are naked in a sauna. Suddenly, there is a beeping sound, which stops when the New Yorker presses his forearm. The two other men look at him.

"That's my pager," the New Yorker explains. "I have a microchip implanted under my skin."

A few minutes later, a cell phone rings. The Californian man lifts his palm to his ear. When he is finished his conversation, he says to his naked companions, "That was my phone; it's implanted under my skin."

The cowboy is feeling very low-tech, but he is determined not to be outdone. He leaves the sauna and goes into the bathroom. He returns a few minutes later with a long piece of toilet paper hanging from his butt.

"Whaddaya know!" he exclaims. "Someone's sending me a fax!"

Takin' a Test

A young cowboy reports for his university final exam that consists of yes-no type of questions. He takes his seat in the examination hall and stares at the exam for five minutes. In a fit of inspiration, he takes out his wallet, removes a coin, starts tossing the coin up in the air and then makes a mark on the answer sheet: he marks "yes" for heads and "no" for tails.

Within half an hour he is done the exam, while the rest of the class is still sweating it out.

The moderator of the exam then watches as the cowboy desperately throws the coin up in the air again, muttering to himself. The moderator asks him what he is doing.

The cowboy replies, "I finished the exam in a half hour, but I'm rechecking my answers."

Poor Folks

One afternoon, a wealthy lawyer is riding in the back of his limousine when he sees two cowboys eating grass by the roadside. He orders his driver to stop, and the lawyer gets out to investigate.

"Why are you eating grass?" he asks one of the men.

"We don't have any money for food," the poor cowboy replies.

"Oh, come along with me then."

"But sir, I have a wife and two children!"

"Bring them along! And you, come with us too!" he says to the other man.

"But sir, I have a wife and six children!" the second cowboy says.

"Bring them as well!"

The two cowboys and their wives and children all climb into the car, which is no easy task, even for a car as large as the limo.

Once underway, one of the cowboys says, "Sir, you are too kind. Thank you for taking all of us with you."

The lawyer replies, "No problem. The grass at my home is about two feet tall!"

Tips on How to be a Cowboy in the Modern World

1. Pull your pants up. You look like an idiot.

2. Turn your cap right; your head ain't crooked.

3. Let's get this straight: it's called a gravel road. I drive a pickup truck because I want to. No matter how slow you drive, you're gonna get dust on your Lexus. Drive, or get out of the way.

4. They are cattle. That's why they smell like cattle. It's the smell of money to us. Get over it. Don't like it? I-10 and I-40 go east and west; I-17 and I-15 go north and south. Pick one and go.

5. So you have a $60,000 car. We're impressed. We have $250,000 combines that we drive only three weeks a year.

6. Every person in the Wild West waves. It's called being friendly. Try to understand the concept.

7. If that cell phone rings while a bunch of geese/pheasants/ducks/doves are coming in during a hunt, we will shoot the dang thing outta your hand. You better hope you don't have it up to your ear at the time.

8. Yeah. We eat trout, salmon, deer and elk. You really want sushi and caviar? It's available at the corner bait shop.

9. "The Opener" refers to the first day of deer season. It's a religious holiday held the closest Saturday to the first of November.

10. We open doors for women. That applies to all women, regardless of age.

11. No, there's no vegetarian special on the menu. Order steak, or you can order the Chef Salad and pick off the two pounds of ham and turkey.

12. When we fill out a table, there are three main dishes: meat, vegetables and bread. We use three spices: salt, pepper and ketchup. Oh, yeah, by the way, we don't care what you folks in Cincinnati call that stuff you eat—it ain't real chili!

13. You bring coke into my house, it better be brown, wet and served over ice. You bring Mary Jane into my house, she better be cute, know how to ride a horse, drive a truck and have long hair.

14. College and high school football is as important here in the West as the Giants, the Yankees, the Mets, the Lakers and the Knicks, and a dang sight more fun to watch.

15. Yeah, we have golf courses out West, too. But don't hit the ball into our yards—it spooks the horses.

16. Turn down that blasted car stereo! That thumpity-thump ain't music, anyway. We don't want to hear it anymore than we want to see your boxers! Refer back to number one!

CHAPTER EIGHT

Cowboy Love

Close Shave

A cowboy walks into a barbershop, sits in the barber's chair and says, "I'll have a shave and a shoe shine."

The barber begins to lather the cowboy's face while a woman with the biggest, firmest, most beautiful breasts that the cowboy has ever seen kneels down and starts to shine his boots.

The cowboy says, "Young lady, you and I should go and spend some time in a hotel room."

She replies, "I'm married, and my husband wouldn't like that."

The cowboy says, "Tell him you're working overtime, and I'll pay you the difference."

"Tell him yourself. He's the one shaving you," the woman replies.

Virtuous

A cowboy asks his buddy to go with him to a traveling stage show to see a beautiful concert singer.

"Is she any good?" asks his friend.

"Good? Why, man, she's a virtuoso!"

"To hell with her morals," his friend snorts. "I just want to know if she can sing!"

Blond Cowboy

The sheriff in a small town walks out in the street and sees a blond cowboy coming down the sidewalk wearing nothing but his cowboy hat, gun and boots, so the lawman arrests him for indecent exposure.

As he is locking him up, the sheriff asks, "Why in the world are you dressed like this?"

The cowboy says, "Well, it's like this, sheriff…I was in the bar down the road and this pretty little redhead asks me to go out to her motor home with her…so I did. We go inside, and she takes off her top and asks me to pull off my shirt, so I did. Then she takes off her skirt and asks me to pull off my jeans, so I did. Then she removes her panties and asks me to pull off my underwear, so I did. Then she gets on the bed, gives me a sexy look and says, 'Now go downtown, cowboy…' And here I am."

Cowboy Wisdom
If you don't know how to run it, leave it alone.

Confused Cowboy

An old cowboy who is dressed to kill—wearing a cowboy shirt, hat, jeans, spurs and chaps—goes into a bar and orders a whiskey. As he sips his drink, a young lady sits down next to him.

After she orders her drink, she turns to the cowboy and asks him, "Are you a real cowboy?"

He replies, "Well, I've spent my whole life on the ranch, herding cows, breaking horses and mending fences, so I guess I am."

"I've never been on a ranch," says the woman. "I am a lesbian, and I spend my whole day thinking about women. I get up in the morning thinking of women. I think of women when I eat, shower, watch television—everything makes me think of women."

A short while later, the woman leaves the bar, and the cowboy orders another drink. A couple sits down next to him and asks, "Are you a real cowboy?"

"I always thought I was," he answers, "but I just found out that I'm a lesbian."

Honeymoon

A Texan and his bride go into a hotel and ask the hotel desk clerk for a room. The cowboy tells the clerk that they just got married that morning.

"Congratulations!" replies the clerk. "Would you like the bridal then?"

"Nah, thanks," says the cowboy. "I reckon I'll just hold her by the ears 'til she gets the hang of it."

Umm, Honey?

One day a young cowboy and cowgirl decide to get married. He is a man of the world. She is an innocent bride with no experience. After the wedding, they leave for their honeymoon. While driving down the road to get to their hotel, the new bride sees two cows having sex.

Did you know that during branding, cowboys have sore calves?

She asks her husband, "What are them cows up to, honey?"

The husband, a bit flustered, answers, "Why, can't you see? Them cows, they're roping!"

She replies, "Oh, I see!"

After a few more hours of driving, they pass two horses having sex. Again the bride asks, "What are them horses doing, honey?"

The husband answers again, "Them horses, they're roping!"

She replies, "Oh, I see!"

Finally, the newlyweds arrive at their hotel. They wash up and get ready for bed. When the couple gets into bed, they start to explore each other's bodies. Things are going along fine until the bride discovers her husband's penis.

"Oh my!" she cries. "What is that?"

"Well, darlin'," he chuckles proudly, "that's ma rope!"

She slides her hands down farther and gasps, "Oh, my goodness! What are those?" she asks.

"Honey, those're my knots!" he answers.

Finally, the couple begins to make love. After several minutes, the bride says, "Stop, honey, wait a minute!"

Her husband, panting a little, asks, "What's the matter, honey, am I hurting you?"

"No," the bride replies. "Undo them dang knots— I need more rope!"

Cheating Husband

A cowboy is on his deathbed, and his wife is sitting by his side. They have spent a life together out in open country, and it looks like the Lord has finally come for the old man.

The man says to his wife, "Hon, I have to tell you something, I reckon."

The wife replies, "Yes, you can tell me anything."

"I slept with your sister," says the husband.

The wife replies, "Yes, I know."

"And your ma, too," says the dying man.

"I know," says the wife. She then puts a finger to his mouth and says, "Shhh, I know, my darling. Now just relax and let the poison work."

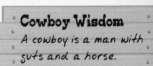

Cowboy Wisdom
A cowboy is a man with guts and a horse.

Do I Know You?

A cowboy is walking down the street when a beautiful woman approaches him.

"Hello," she says with a big bright smile.

He is taken aback and can't place her. "Do I know you?" he asks.

"I think you're the father of one of my kids," she says.

He thinks really hard of who it could be but cannot remember a time when he was unfaithful to his wife.

"Wow," the cowboy says, "are you that stripper from my bachelor party who tied me down on the pool table and did it with me with all my buddies cheering, while your friend sprayed whipped cream on my butt? Boy, that was insane!"

"No," she says with a look of disgust. "I think I'm your son's biology teacher."

Daddy!

In the backcountry out on the plains, a cowboy's pregnant wife goes into labor in the middle of the night, and the doctor is called out to assist in the delivery.

Since they have no electricity, the doctor hands the father-to-be a lantern and says, "Here. Hold this high so I can see what I am doing."

Soon, a baby boy enters the world, and the new father starts to lower the lantern.

"Whoa, there," says the doctor. "Don't be in such a rush to put that lantern down. I think there's another one coming."

Sure enough, within minutes, the doctor delivers a baby girl. "Hold that lantern up! Don't set it down—there's another one!" says the doctor.

Within a few minutes, another baby girl arrives. "No, no, don't be in a hurry to put down that lantern yet. It seems there's another one coming!" cries the doctor.

The cowboy scratches his head in bewilderment and says to the doctor, "You reckon it might be the light that's attractin' 'em?"

Draw!

Two cowboys in the middle of the street are about to duel:

First cowboy: "I am the fastest hand in the West!"

Second cowboy: "I have a girlfriend."

Wrong Bar

A cowboy walks into a bar, and before he gets two steps in, he realizes it's a gay bar.

"What the heck," he says to himself. "I really need a drink."

When the gay waiter approaches, he says to the cowboy, "What's the name of your penis?"

The cowboy says, "Look, I'm not into any of that. All I want is a drink."

> **Cowboy Wisdom**
> Never miss a good chance to shut up.

The gay waiter says, "I'm sorry, but I can't serve you until you tell me the name of your penis. Mine, for example, is called 'Nike,' for the slogan 'Just Do It.' That guy down at the end of the bar calls his 'Snickers' because it really satisfies."

The cowboy looks dumbfounded so the waiter tells him he'll give him a few seconds to think of a name.

The cowboy turns to the man sitting to his left who is drinking a beer and says, "Hey, bud, what's the name of yours?"

The man looks at the cowboy and says with a smile, "Timex."

The thirsty cowboy asks, "Why Timex?"

The fella proudly replies, "'Cause it takes a lickin' and keeps on tickin'!"

A little shaken, the cowboy turns to the two fellas on his right, who happen to be sharing a fruity Margarita, and asks, "So, what do you guys call yours?"

The first man turns to the cowboy and proudly exclaims, "'Ford', because quality is job one." Then he adds, "Have you driven a Ford lately?"

The second guy says, "I call mine 'Chevy'…like a rock!" And he gives the cowboy a wink.

Even more shaken by all this, the cowboy has to think for a moment before he comes up with a name for his manhood. Finally, the waiter returns, and the cowboy exclaims, "The name of my penis is Secret! Now give me a damn beer!"

The waiter brings him a beer, and with a puzzled look on his face, he asks, "Why Secret?"

The cowboy says, "Because it's strong enough for a man but made for a woman!"

Love Is Blind

A cowboy and his cowgirl are horsing around in the forest like lovers do on a sunny day. He is chasing after her when suddenly she screams out, "Watch out for that cliff!"

The cowboy looks back and shouts, "What cli

                i

                   i

                      i

                       f!"

Beer Goggles

Three cowboys are getting drunk at a bar in a hotel. One of the cowboys demands a prostitute from the bartender. The bartender goes to the supply shop and desperately asks the clerk for a prostitute. Although the clerk doesn't know a prostitute, he gives the bartender a life-sized inflatable doll.

Q: Why are horses bad dancers?

A: They have two left feet.

The bartender takes it to the second floor of the hotel, blows it up and lays the doll on the bed. When he returns to the bar, he tells the cowboys that the prostitute is upstairs.

The first cowboy, who is the smallest of the three, goes upstairs first and stays there for 10 minutes, after which he comes back down to the bar.

When asked by the other two cowboys about how she was, he replies, "She had a firm body, but she sure didn't say much." They laugh, and the second cowboy, a medium-sized man, goes upstairs.

> **Cowboy Wisdom**
> The quickest way to double your money is to fold it over and put it back in your pocket.

Upon his arrival in the bar afterward, he is asked the same question, to which he gives the same answer as the first cowboy. The third cowboy, the biggest of the men, goes upstairs, and two minutes later, he comes down with a dazed expression on his face.

"What happened?" the other cowboys ask him.

"Well, when I got on top of her, she suddenly farted and jumped out the window!"

What's in a Name?

A cowboy asks an old Indian what his wife's name is.

He replies, "Wife name is Three Horse."

"That's an unusual name for your wife," says the cowboy. "What does it mean?"

"Is old Indian name. Means 'Nag, Nag, Nag.'"

Love in a Cave

Two Indians and a cowboy are walking along in the bush when, all of a sudden, one of the Indians takes off and runs up a hill to the mouth of a cave.

He stops and hollers into the cave, "Woooo! Woooo! Woooo!"

He listens closely until he hears the answer, "Woooo! Woooo! Woooo!" He then tears off his clothes and runs into the cave.

The cowboy is puzzled and asks the other Indian what that was all about and whether the fellow is nuts or something.

"No," says the other Indian. "It is mating time for us Indians, and when we see a cave and holler, "Woooo! Woooo! Woooo!" and get an answer back, that means a woman is in the cave waiting for us."

Well, just about that time, the second Indian sees another cave. He takes off and runs up to the cave, then stops and hollers, "Woooo! Woooo! Woooo!" When he hears the return, "Woooo! Woooo! Woooo!" off come his clothes and into the cave he goes.

The cowboy starts running around looking for a cave to find these women that the Indians talked about. All of a sudden, he looks up and sees a great big cave. As he looks at the cave in amazement, he thinks to himself, "Man! Look at the size of that cave! It's bigger than the ones those Indians found. There must be a really great woman in this cave!"

He runs up the hill at a super fast speed, gets in front of the cave and hollers, "Wooooo! Wooooo! Wooooo!" The cowboy is tickled all over when he hears the very loud answering call of, "Wooooooooooo! Wooooooooooo!! Wooooooooooo!" Off come his clothes and, with a big smile on his face, he races into the cave.

The next day in the newspaper, the headline reads, "Naked Cowboy Run Over by Freight Train."

In Mourning—Sort of

A cowboy is drinking heavily in a bar.

"I think you've had too much," says the bartender.

The cowboy gets angry and says, "I just lost my wife!"

The bartender looks at him with sympathy and says, "It must be hard losing your wife."

"Hard? It was damn near impossible."

Daisy

A cowboy sits quietly reading his morning paper one Sunday morning. Suddenly, he is knocked almost senseless by his wife, who stands behind him holding a frying pan in her hand.

> **Cowboy Wisdom**
> Never drive black cattle in the dark.

Cowboy: "What was that for?"

Wife: "Why do you have a piece of paper in your pocket with 'Daisy' written on it?"

Cowboy: "Oh, honey, don't you remember two weeks ago when I went to the rodeo? Daisy was the name of the horse I rode on."

The wife is satisfied with his answer and apologizes for bonking him.

Three days later, he is sitting reading the paper when once again he is bonked on the head.

Cowboy: "What's that for this time?"

Wife: "Your horse called."

The Mind of Custer

An eccentric billionaire wants a mural painted on his library wall, so he calls an artist.

Describing what he wants, the billionaire says, "I am a history buff, and I want your interpretation of the last thing that went through Custer's mind before he died. I am going out of town on business for a week, and when I return, I expect to see the mural completed."

Upon his return, the billionaire goes to the library to examine the finished artwork. To his surprise, he finds a painting of a cow with a halo. Surrounding this are hundreds of Indians in various sexual positions.

Furious, he calls the artist back to his home. "What the hell is this?" screams the billionaire, pointing at the mural.

"Why, that's exactly what you asked for," replies the artist smugly.

"No! I didn't ask for a mural of pornographic filth. I asked for an interpretation of Custer's last thoughts!"

"And there you have it," says the artist. "I call it, 'Holy Cow, Look at all Those F***ing Indians.'"

In-laws

A recently married cowboy is having some mother-in-law issues. His mother-in-law nags him every day and tells him he is a no-good cowboy too ugly for her daughter. His buddy invites him out for a night on the town so that the cowboy can drown his sorrows.

The cowboy says, "It wouldn't work. She can swim!"

Drinker with Reason

A cowboy walks into a saloon and orders a double shot of bourbon. He chugs it down, reaches into his pocket and pulls out a photograph. After staring at the picture for a few moments, he puts it away and orders a double whiskey.

When he finishes downing that drink, he pulls out the photo again, looks at it for a few moments, puts it back in his pocket, then orders another double. He repeats this process over and over again for more than an hour.

Finally, the bartender becomes curious and says, "Excuse me, pardner. Why after every drink do you keep staring at that photo?"

"It's a picture of my wife," explains the now-drunk cowboy, "and when she starts to look good, I'm going home."

Tombstone

A Texas couple has a furious fight on their 25th wedding anniversary. The rancher is so angry at his wife that he goes out and buys her with a gift of a tombstone with the inscription reading, "Here Lies My Wife—Cold as Ever."

In retaliation, the wife goes out the next day and buys her husband a tombstone with the inscription that says, "Here Lies My Husband—Stiff at Last."

At the Altar

At the wedding rehearsal of a young couple, the cowpoke takes the minister aside and says to him, "I'll give you 100 dollars if you change my wedding vows. When you reach the part where I promise to love, honor and obey, and especially the part about forsaking all others and being faithful to her forever, do you think you could forget that part?"

When the minister replies that he can do that, the groom walks away feeling good about himself.

At the ceremony the next day, the minister gets to the groom's vows and says, "Do you promise to obey her every command and wish, serve her breakfast in

Q: What do you get from nervous cows?

A: Milkshakes.

bed every morning and swear that you will never look at another woman?"

The groom is shocked. "I thought we had a deal?" he whispers to the minister.

"Yes," replies the minister, "but the bride made me a better offer."

Bar Story

A cowboy walks into a bar with his arm in a cast. "What happened to you?" asks the bartender.

"I got into a fight with Jesse."

"Jesse? He's only a small guy—he must have had something in his hand."

"He did—a shovel."

"Didn't you have anything in your hand?"

"I did—Mrs. Jesse's panties. And as lovely as they were, they ain't much use in a fight."

Lonely

Out on the plains of the American West, a lonely woman has been sitting at home for years, never able to attract a husband. Out of desperation, she puts an ad in several newspapers looking for her dream man. She writes that she wants a cowboy who will not beat her up, not run away from her and who must be great in bed.

Weeks go by with no replies, and she almost gives up hope when one day she hears her doorbell ring. She opens the door and sees a man wearing a cowboy hat with no arms and no legs lying on the doormat.

"Who are you?" she asks.

"I'm your dream man," he replies.

"What makes you think you fit the mold I'm looking for?"

"I'm a cowboy with no arms so I can't beat you, and I've got no legs so I can't run away," he replies.

"What makes you think you're going to be great in bed?" she asks.

"Well, I rang the doorbell, didn't I?"

"Come in!"

Cowboy Gold

After striking gold in the mountains of Montana, a miner heads straight for the nearest bar and announces, "I'm lookin' for the meanest, roughest, toughest whore in town."

The bartender says, "I reckon we can help you. She's upstairs—second room on the right."

The miner hands the bartender a gold nugget to pay for the girl, grabs two beer bottles and marches upstairs. He flings open the door to the room and says, "I'm lookin' for the meanest, roughest, toughest whore in town."

"Well, you found her," says the woman. Then she strips naked, bends over and grabs her ankles.

The miner says, "How did you know I want it in that position?"

"I didn't, but I thought you might like to open those beers first."

Daddy's Girls

An old cowboy has three pretty teenage daughters of whom he is very fond and extremely protective. He sits on his front porch, shotgun in hand, and runs his eyes over any man who comes to court one of his daughters. If he doesn't like the look of them, he sends them running with a shot over their heads.

One night, all three girls are waiting on their dates.

The first girl's boyfriend drives up and says to the father, "Hi, my name is Joe. I'm here to get Flo, and we're going to the show. Is she ready to go?"

The old cowboy decides that the boy sounds okay and gives his blessing by not shooting at him.

Ten minutes later, another car pulls up. The driver gets out and says, "Hi, my name is Freddy. I'm here to get Betty, and we're going for spaghetti. Is she ready?"

The old man thinks the boy is nice and gives his permission.

Cowboy Wisdom
Generally, you ain't learnin' nothing when your mouth's a-jawin'.

Ten minutes later, the last car arrives. The driver gets out and says, "Hi, my name is Chuck…"

And the old cowboy shoots him.

Two Cowboy Neighbors

A cowboy corners his neighbor at the end of his driveway. "Hey, Dwayne, do you like a woman with a big stomach?"

"No, I don't," says Dwayne, thinking the question is a little odd.

"Do you like a woman whose breasts sag so much that they almost touch her feet?"

"No, I don't," says Dwayne.

"Do you like a woman whose hips are as wide as a horse?"

"Heck, no, I don't!"

"Well, then," says the cowboy. "Keep yer dang hands off my wife!"

Cow Love

A Texas cowgirl buys a cow for her family's milk supply. The cow provides a lot of milk and is so profitable that the cowgirl decides to try to breed her. She rides into town and buys a bull from a rancher.

When she gets home, she puts the cow and bull together expecting instant results, but the bull isn't interested in the cow. The bull just spends the whole day stomping around the ranch.

Frustrated, the cowgirl takes the bull to a local veterinarian and explains the problem to see if there is something wrong with the animal.

"Did this bull come from New Mexico?" asks the lady vet.

"As a matter of fact it did. Why do you ask?" replies the cowgirl.

"Because my husband is from New Mexico!"

Escaped Husband

After serving 18 months of a 25-year sentence, the meanest, dirtiest killer in the Wild West escapes from prison. It is the talk of every county, and the local sheriff mobilizes a huge posse to look for him.

Knowing he is a wanted man, the escaped prisoner is careful making his way home—he crosses through all the backcountry, through forests and across rivers.

When he finally makes it to his house, he looks around to make sure the coast is clear before he knocks on the door.

His wife opens the door. "You dirty rat!" she screams. "Where have you been? You escaped two days ago!"

Grief

A man places some flowers on the grave of his dearly departed mother and starts to walk away when his attention is diverted by a cowboy kneeling at a grave.

The cowboy seems to be praying with profound intensity and keeps repeating, "Why did you have to die? Why did you have to die?"

The man approaches the cowboy and says, "Sir, I don't wish to intrude on your private grief, but this demonstration of pain is more than I've ever seen before. For whom do you mourn so deeply? A child? A parent?"

The cowboy takes a moment to collect himself, then replies, "My wife's first husband."

Positions

Two cowboys in a bar are discussing sexual positions. The older cowboy says to the young, naive cowboy, "My favorite is the rodeo!"

The young cowboy says, "What's the rodeo?"

"Well, first you get your wife down and start to do her doggy style, then when you're halfway done, you bend over and whisper in her ear, 'You know, this is your sister's favorite position, too,' and then you try to hold on for eight seconds!"

Q: What does it mean if you find a horseshoe?

A: Some poor horse is walking around in its socks.

Dada

A middle-aged couple has two beautiful daughters. For the longest time, the father has complained that he never had a son. He wanted to teach his son the ways of men, and he wanted him to help on the ranch and grow into a strong cowboy. So he and his wife decide to try one last time for the son they always wanted.

Soon, the wife gets pregnant, and nine months later, delivers a baby boy.

The joyful father rushes to the nursery to see his new son but is horrified to find an incredibly ugly baby.

He goes to his wife and says, "I cannot possibly be the father of that hideous child. Look at the two beautiful daughters I fathered."

When his wife blushes, the husband gets suspicious and demands, "Have you been fooling around on me?"

His wife says, "Not this time."

Happy Marriage

Two cowboys are riding their horses in the backcountry and stop at a bar for a drink. All of a sudden, Bill says, "I think I'm going to divorce my wife—she hasn't spoken to me in over six months."

Earl sips his beer and says, "You better think it over—women like that are hard to find."

Double the Fun

An old cowboy is in a cave looking for treasure. He finds an old lamp and rubs it, and a genie appears.

The genie says, "I will grant you three wishes, but your ex-wife will get double."

The man agrees and says, "I wish I had a mansion."

The genie grants the wish, and the cowboy's ex-wife gets two mansions.

The man says, "I would like one million dollars."

The genie again grants the wish, and the ex-wife gets $2 million.

Then the cowboy says, "Scare me half to death."

Motive

A cowboy is on trial for killing his wife after he finds her in bed with a neighbor. When his lawyer asks why he shot his wife instead of her lover, the cowboy replies, "Is it not better to shoot the woman once than a different man every week?"

Honeymooners

A young cowboy and his beautiful bride on their honeymoon check into a hotel and go up to their room. After a few minutes, the desk clerk sees the man walking downstairs with his tackle box and fishing pole.

Cowboy Wisdom
Basketball, football, baseball...Rodeo! Bring yer own balls!

The man walks out the door and is gone until nearly midnight.

Before dawn the next morning, once again the desk clerk sees the man walking out the door with his fishing pole and tackle box. He is gone all day and returns really late.

On the third day, as the man walks down the stairs with his tackle box and fishing pole, the desk clerk stops him.

"Excuse me, sir, but I understand you are on your honeymoon," he says.

"Yes, sir," the man replies.

"Well, if my wife looked like that, I'd be upstairs in bed with her," he says.

"I can't—she has gonorrhea." the man replies casually.

"Okay, how 'bout a little oral action?"

"Nope, she's got herpes," the man says calmly.

Agitated, the desk clerk says, "Well, you could take the back door."

"Nope, she's got diarrhea."

Frustrated, the desk clerk shouts, "Well, then why the hell did you marry her?"

The man smiles and says, "She's got worms too, and they make good bait."

Kin

Two cowboys from Tennessee are sitting around talking one afternoon.

After a while, the first cowboy says to the second, "If'n I was to sneak over to your trailer Saturday and make love to your wife while you was off rustlin' cattle, and she got pregnant and had a baby, would that make us kin?"

The second cowboy crooks his head sideways for a minute, scratches his head and squints his eyes, thinking real hard about the question. Finally, he says, "Well, I don't know about that, but it sure would make us even."

Best Buds

An old cowboy is sitting at the bar in his local saloon, furiously imbibing shots of whiskey. One of his good friends happens to come into the bar and sees him.

"Lou," says the shocked friend, "what are you doing? I've known you for more than 15 years, and I've never seen you take a drink before. What's going on?"

Without even taking his eyes off his newly filled shot glass, the man replies, "My wife just ran off with my best friend." He then throws back another shot of whisky in one gulp.

"But," says the other man, "I'm your best friend!"

The man turns to his friend, looks at him through bloodshot eyes, smiles and then slurs, "Not anymore! He is!"

Hot Lady

Q: Why did the train robber take a bath?

A: He wanted to make a clean getaway!

Jeff walks into a saloon one night and sees his friend Paul slumped over the bar. Jeff walks over and asks Paul what's wrong.

"Well," replies Paul, "you know that beautiful girl at work that I wanted to ask out, but I get an erection every time I see her?"

"Yes," replies Jeff with a laugh.

"Well," says Paul, straightening up, "I finally worked up the courage to ask her out, and she agreed."

"That's great!" says Jeff. "When are you going out?"

"I went to meet her earlier this evening," continues Paul, "but I was worried I'd get an erection again. So I got some duct tape and taped my penis to my leg, so that if I did get hard, it wouldn't show."

"Sensible," replies Jeff.

"So I get to her door," says Paul, "and I ring her doorbell. She opens the door and is wearing the sheerest, sexiest dress you ever saw."

"And what happened then?"

"I kicked her in the face."

Leather

When a woman wears leather clothing, a cowboy's heart beats quicker, his throat gets dry, he gets weak in the knees and he begins to think irrationally.

Ever wonder why?

Because she smells like a new saddle.

Lookin' fer Love

A handsome blond cowboy is looking for a bride when he comes across a rancher with three gorgeous blonde daughters. The young cowboy can't decide which daughter to have for his wife so he takes each one out in turn. After taking out the first daughter, the rancher asks the cowboy for his opinion.

"Well," says the cowboy, "she's just a wee bit—not that you could hardly tell—knock-kneed."

The cowboy then takes out the second daughter, and again the rancher asks for the cowboy's thoughts. "Well, she's just a wee bit—not that you could hardly tell—cross-eyed."

The cowboy then takes out the third daughter, and the next morning he rushes over to the rancher's home and screams out, "She's perfect, just perfect! She is the one I will marry."

The rancher's daughter and the cowboy marry, but six months later, she gives birth to an ugly, redheaded baby. The cowboy goes back to the rancher demanding an explanation for what has happened.

"Well," explains the rancher. "When you met her, she was just a wee bit—not that you could hardly tell—pregnant."

Just Like Dad

A bride, upon her engagement, goes to her mother and says, "I've found a man just like father!"

Her mother replies, "So what do you want from me—sympathy?"

Free at Last!

Cowboy Bad Bernie has been in prison for seven years. The day he gets out, his wife and young son are there to pick him up. He walks through the prison gates and gets into the carriage.

The only thing he says is, "F.F."

His wife turns to him and answers, "E.F."

Out on the trail, he says again, "F.F."

She responds simply: "E.F."

He repeats, "F.F."

She again replies, "E.F."

"Mom! Dad!" their son yells. "What's going on?"

Bad Bernie answers, "Your mother wants to eat first."

Honey, I'm Home!

Every night after dinner, Cowboy Harry takes off for the local saloon. He spends the whole evening there and always arrives home, well inebriated, around midnight each night. He usually has trouble getting his key to fit the keyhole and can't get the door open. And every time this happens, his wife goes to the door and lets him in. Then she proceeds to scream at him for his constant nights out and coming home in a drunken state. But Harry still continues his nightly routine.

One day, the distraught wife is talking to a friend about her husband's behavior. The friend listens and then says, "Why don't you treat him a little differently when he comes home? Instead of berating him, why don't you give him some loving words and welcome him home with a kiss? Then he might change his ways." The wife thinks that this might be a good idea.

> **Q:** What's the slowest horse in the world?
>
> **A:** A clotheshorse.

That night, Harry takes off again after dinner. And at about midnight, he arrives home in his usual condition.

His wife hears him at the door. She quickly opens it and lets Harry in. Instead of berating him like she always does, she takes his arm and leads him into the living room. She sits Harry down in his favorite chair, puts his feet up on the footstool and takes his boots off. Then she goes behind him and starts to cuddle him a little. After a while, she whispers to Harry, "It's pretty late, dear. I think we should go upstairs to bed now, don't you think?"

Cowboy Harry replies in his inebriated state, "Heck, I guess we might as well. I'll get in trouble when I get home anyway!"

Indian's Daughter

A young cowboy is lost and wandering in a forest when he comes upon a small house.

He knocks on the door and is greeted by an ancient Native man.

"I'm lost," says the man. "Can you put me up for the night?"

"Certainly," the old Indian says, "but on one condition. If you so much as lay a finger on my daughter, I will inflict upon you the three worst Indian tortures known to man."

"Okay," says the cowboy, thinking that the daughter must be pretty old as well, and he enters the house.

Before dinner, the daughter comes down the stairs. She is young, beautiful and has a fantastic figure. She is obviously attracted to the cowboy because she can't keep her eyes off him during the meal.

Remembering the old man's warning, the cowboy ignores the daughter during dinner and then goes up to bed alone.

But during he night, he can bear it no longer and sneaks into her bedroom for a night of passion. He is careful to keep their lovemaking quiet so the old man won't hear. Near dawn, the cowboy creeps back to his room, exhausted but happy.

He wakes in the morning with a feeling of pressure on his chest. Opening his eyes, he sees a large rock on his chest with a note on it that reads, "Indian Torture 1: Large rock on chest."

"Well, that's pretty crappy," the cowboy says to himself. "But if that's the best the old man can do, I don't have much to worry about."

He picks up the boulder, walks over to the window and throws the boulder out. As he does so, he suddenly notices another note on the boulder that reads, "Indian Torture 2: Rock tied to left testicle."

In a panic, the cowboy glances down and sees the rope is already getting close to the end.

Figuring that a few broken bones is better than castration, he jumps out of the window after the boulder.

As he plummets downward, he sees a large sign on the ground that reads, "Indian Torture 3: Right testicle tied to bedpost."

How to Impress a Woman

- Compliment her.
- Cuddle her.
- Kiss her.
- Caress her.
- Love her.
- Tease her.
- Comfort her.
- Protect her.
- Hug her.
- Hold her.
- Spend money on her.
- Wine and dine her.
- Buy things for her.
- Listen to her.
- Care for her.
- Stand by her.
- Support her.
- Go to the ends of the earth for her.

How to Impress a Cowboy

- Show up naked.

Young Cowpoke

A young cowboy goes to a whorehouse to experience his first taste of sex.

The madam suggests that he start with 69. He decides to give it a try.

The prostitute leads him to a room, gets undressed and instructs the young man on what to do.

Unfortunately, just as he starts, she farts.

The man quietly says to himself, "Phew," but he goes down on her again.

A moment later, she farts again. He says, "Phew," but continues.

Once more she farts. This time he immediately gets up and starts walking out. She asks him what's wrong, and he replies, "I don't think I can take another 66 of those!"

Psychic

During an outing in Nevada, a married cowgirl sneaks off to visit a fortune-teller of some local repute. In a dark and hazy room, peering into a crystal ball, the mystic delivers grave news. "There's no easy way to say this, so I'll just be blunt: prepare yourself to be a widow. Your husband will die a violent and horrible death this year."

Cowboy Wisdom
Make apologies, not excuses.

Visibly shaken, the cowgirl stares at the fortune-teller's lined face, then at the single flickering candle, then down at her hands. She takes a few deep breaths to compose herself. She simply has to know. She meets the fortune-teller's gaze, steadies her voice and asks, "Will I be acquitted?"

New Bride

A young woman named Sarah marries Cowboy Sam, and they go on their honeymoon. When they return home a week later, the new bride immediately calls her mother.

"Well," says her mother, "how was the honeymoon, darlin'?"

"Oh, Mama," Sarah replies, "the honeymoon was wonderful! So romantic…" Suddenly Sarah bursts out crying. "But, Mama, as soon as we returned, Sam started using the most horrible language—words I never heard before! I mean, all these awful four-letter words! You have to let me come back home. Please, Mama!"

"Sarah, Sarah," her mother says, "calm down! You need to stay with your husband and work this out. Now, tell me, what could be so awful? What four-letter words did he say?"

"Please don't make me tell you, Mama," cries the daughter. "I'm so embarrassed—they're just too awful! Come get me, please!"

"Darlin, baby, you must tell me what has you so upset. Tell your mama these horrible four-letter words!"

Still sobbing, the bride says, "Oh, Mama, he used words like *dust, wash, iron, cook*."

"I'll pick you up in 20 minutes," says the mother.

That's Once

A cowboy and his brand-new bride are riding home from the chapel in a wagon pulled by a team of horses when the older horse stumbles.

The cowboy says, "That's once."

A little farther along, the old horse stumbles again.

The cowboy says, "That's twice."

After a little while longer, the poor old horse stumbles again. The cowboy doesn't say anything but reaches under his seat, pulls out a shotgun and shoots the horse.

His bride yells, "That's an awful thing to do!"

"That's once!"

Chilly Weekend

A couple from Texas goes to Alaska in the fall for a romantic weekend getaway. When they get to their rented cabin, it's so cold that the wife asks her husband to go chop some wood for the fireplace. He comes in after five minutes and tells his wife that his hands are cold. She tells her husband to put his hands between her thighs to warm them.

So he does, and he goes back outside to finish chopping wood. He comes in after another five minutes and says, "Honey, my hands are cold again." So she again tells him to put his hands between her thighs to warm them.

So he does, and then he goes back outside to chop some more wood. Five minutes pass, and he comes in again and says, "Honey, my hands are cold again."

His wife says, "Damn! Don't your ears ever get cold?"

Cheap Grub

A cowboy walks into a saloon one night. He goes up to the bar and asks for a beer.

"Certainly, sir, that'll be one cent," says the bartender.

"One cent!" exclaims the guy.

The barman replies, "Yes."

So the cowboy glances at the menu and says, "Can I have a nice, juicy T-bone steak with fries, peas and a fried egg?"

"Certainly, sir," replies the bartender, "but that will cost you a lot more money."

"How much money?" inquires the cowboy.

"Four cents."

"Four cents!" exclaims the guy. "Where's the man who owns this place?"

The barman replies, "Upstairs with my wife."

The cowboy says, "What's he doing with your wife?"

The bartender replies, "Same as what I'm doing to his business."

Genie Love

A cowboy and his wife are having an argument. Suddenly, the cowboy picks up a bottle lying near him and throws it at his wife. The bottle misses the wife, flies through the open window in the kitchen and hits the neighbor's window, breaking the glass.

Q: Why do you have a cow on your front yard?

A: It's mooing the lawn.

Now, both the husband and wife are embarrassed and go to apologize to the neighbor. Upon reaching the house, they find a young man sitting on a couch with a smile on his face.

Before the couple can say anything, the man says, "I am a genie. I was enclosed in that bottle for many years, but you two have set me free, so ask for any three wishes you want, and it shall be granted. But along with your three wishes, you will have to fulfill one wish of mine."

The couple are so happy that they don't think twice and present their wishes.

"I want millions of dollars in my bank account," says the husband.

"Done," says the genie.

"I want diamond jewelry," says the wife.

"Done," says the genie.

"I want to own houses all over the world," says the husband.

"Done," says the genie.

Now it is time for the genie's wish. "So," the genie says, "I have fulfilled all your three wishes, and it's time for my wish. I have not slept with a woman for a long time. I wish to have sex with your wife."

The couple gets worried, but the husband explains to his wife that it is only a genie, and it doesn't matter much to him. Besides, the genie has given them a lot of things. So the wife consents.

The genie and the wife have a lovely night together.

Finally, in the morning the genie says to the woman, "It was wonderful, but how old is your husband?"

"Why, he is just 35."

"Oh," says the genie, "even at 35 he still believes in genies."

Canadian Couple

An elderly couple, Margaret and Bert, live in Alberta. Bert always wanted a pair of authentic cowboy boots. Seeing some on sale one day, he buys them, wears them home, walking proudly. He walks into the house and says to his wife, "Do you notice anything different about me?"

Margaret looks him over and says, "Nope."

Frustrated, Bert storms off into the bathroom, undresses, and walks back into the room completely naked except for the new boots. Again, a little louder this time, he asks, "Notice anything different *now*?"

Margaret looks up and says, "What's different? It's hanging down today, it was hanging down yesterday and it'll be hanging down again tomorrow."

Furious, Bert yells, "And do you know *why* it's hanging down, Margaret!?'

"Nope," she replies.

"It's hanging down because it's looking at my new boots!"

To which Margaret replies, "Shoulda bought a hat, Bert. Shoulda bought a hat."

CHAPTER NINE

All Work and No Play

Blacksmith

A tough-looking cowboy is strutting down the main drag of a sleepy little town when he happens into a blacksmith's shop and finds a very large blacksmith making horseshoes.

To not appear intimidated, the cowboy reaches for a finished horseshoe in a barrel next to the blacksmith. The blacksmith starts to stop him, but the cowboy scowls and continues to examine the horseshoe.

Burning his hand severely, the cowboy quickly throws the horseshoe back into the barrel.

The blacksmith snickers and says, "Hot, aren't they?"

The cowboy replies, "No, it just don't take me very long to look at a horseshoe."

Visitor on the Range

A man is passing by a pasture and sees a beautiful horse. Hoping to buy the animal, he finds the owner and says to the cowboy, "I think your horse looks pretty good, so I'll give you $500 for him."

"He doesn't look so good, and he's not for sale," replies the cowboy.

The man says, "I think he looks just fine, and I'll up the price to $1000."

"He doesn't look so good," repeats the cowboy, "but if you want him that much, he's yours."

The next day, the man returns to see the cowboy. He goes up to the cowboy and screams, "You sold me a blind horse! You cheated me!"

The cowboy calmly replies, "I told you he didn't look so good, didn't I?"

Hot Days

In a small town in Nevada, it gets so hot that the sheriff likes to walk around bare-chested, sans shirt, if you will.

When asked what the hardest part of his job is, he replies, "Pinning on my badge!"

New Sheriff in Town

On his first day on the job, the new sheriff walks around his town and finds evidence everywhere that an amazing sharpshooter has been practicing. Wherever he looks—on walls, fences, empty cans—there are bull's eyes with bullet holes through the center of the targets. After asking a few of the locals, he finally learns the identity of the mystery sharpshooter and finds the man so he can introduce himself.

Cowboy Wisdom
Don't build the gate until you build the corral.

"Mister, that's the finest shooting I've ever seen," the sheriff says to the cowboy. "How do you do it?"

"Why, it's simple, sheriff," replies the cowboy. "I shoot first, then I draw the circles."

Something Ain't Right

Back in the old Wild West, two blond cowpokes, Jeff and Dave are enjoying a whiskey in the local saloon when a man walks in with an Indian's head under his arm.

The barman shakes his hand and says, "I hate Indians. Last week they burnt my barn to the ground, assaulted my wife and killed my children."

He then says, "If any man brings me the head of an Indian, I'll give him 1000 dollars."

The two cowboys look at each other and walk out of the bar to go hunting for an Indian. They walk around for a while when suddenly they see an Indian guy riding a horse. Jeff throws a rock, and it hits the Indian right on the forehead. The Indian falls off his horse and lands 70 feet down a ravine.

The two cowboys make their way down the ravine where Dave pulls out a knife to claim their trophy.

Suddenly, Jeff says, "Dave, take a look at this."

Dave replies, "Not now, I'm busy."

Jeff tugs on Dave's shirt and says, "I really think you should look at this."

Dave says, "Look, you can see I'm busy. There's 1000 dollars in my hand."

Q: What's the last thing you hear before a cowboy dies?

A: "Hey, y'all watch this!"

But Jeff is adamant. "Please, Dave, take a look at this."

So Dave looks up and sees that standing at the top of the ravine are 5000 Indians.

Dave just shakes his head and says, "Oh my God, we're going to be millionaires!"

Ouch

A rancher with five arrows stuck in his back walks into a doctor's office.

He says, "Doc, can you help me?"

"Now, let's see," says the doc. "Tell me where it hurts exactly."

Two Deputies

On a warm summer night, two deputies are patrolling the town on foot. One says to the other, "What's wrong, Jim? Why are you shaking like that?"

"I just came out of the butcher's cold room!" replies Jim.

"What the heck were you doing in der?"

"Didn't the sheriff tell you?" says Jim with a shiver. "He says he wanted us to be cold-blooded lawmen."

Traffic

Two cowboys come upon an Indian man lying on his stomach with his ear to the ground. One of the cowboys stops and says to the other, "You see that Indian?"

"Yeah," says the other cowboy.

"Look," says the first man, "He's listening to the ground. He can hear things for miles in any direction."

Just then the Indian looks up. "Covered wagon," he says, "about two miles away. Have two horses—one brown, one white. Man, woman, child, furniture in wagon."

"Incredible!" says the cowboy to his friend. "This Indian knows how far away the wagon is, how many horses it has, what color they are and who and what is in the wagon. Amazing!"

The Indian looks up again and says, "Ran over me about a half hour ago."

Headquarters

On a quiet night at the sheriff's office, a man bursts through the door and says, "You have to arrest me!"

"Why? What did you do?" asks the sheriff.

"I emptied six rounds on my wife!" replies the man.

"You killed your wife? You dang varmint!" says the sheriff, drawing his pistol.

"No, every bullet missed," says the man. "That's why you have to lock me up so she can't get to me."

For Hire

A successful rancher dies and leaves all his possessions to his beautiful, devoted wife. The widow is determined to keep the ranch. However, she knows little about ranching so she places an ad in the newspaper for a ranch hand.

Two men apply for the job. One man is gay, and the other is a drunk. The woman thinks long and hard about which man to hire, and when no one else applies for the job, she hires the gay guy, figuring it will be safer to have him around the house than the drunk.

Cowboy Wisdom
Never pass up on good shade.

The new ranch hand proves to be a hard worker who puts in long hours every day and knows a lot about ranching.

One day, the widow says to the hired hand, "You've done a really good job, and the ranch looks great. You should go into town and kick up your heels."

The hired hand readily agrees and goes into town that Saturday night. However, one o'clock comes, and he hasn't returned home. Two o'clock, and no hired hand. He arrives home around two-thirty and finds the widow sitting by the fireplace. She quietly calls him over to her.

"Unbutton my blouse and take it off," she says.

Trembling, the hired hand does as she directs.

"Now, take off my boots."

He does so, slowly.

"Now, take off my socks."

He does.

"Now, take off my skirt."

He does.

"Now, take off my bra."

Again, with trembling hands, he does as he is told.

"Now," she says, "take off my panties." He slowly pulls them down and off.

Then she looks at him and says, "If you ever wear my clothes to town again, I'll fire you on the spot!"

Accident on the Farm

A young farm boy accidentally overturns his wagon-load of corn while traveling down a country road. The rancher who lives nearby hears the noise.

"Hey, Willis!" the rancher yells. "Forget your troubles. Come in and eat dinner with us. Then I'll help you get the wagon back up."

"That's mighty nice of you," Willis answers, "but I don't think Pa would like me to."

"Nonsense, come on!" the rancher insists.

"Well, okay," the boy finally agrees, "but Pa won't like it."

After eating a hearty dinner, Willis thanks his host. "I feel a lot better now, but I know Pa is going to be real upset."

"Don't be foolish!" the rancher says with a smile. "By the way, where is your pa?"

"Under the wagon."

Sleeping Arrangements

Four cowboys traveling together across Utah decide to stay a few days in a small two-room cabin, where they sleep two to a room. No one wants to room with Daryl because he snores so loudly. They don't think it's fair to make one of them stay with him the whole time, so they vote to take turns.

Cowboy Wisdom
Beauty is in the eye of the beer holder.

The first cowboy sleeps with Daryl and comes to breakfast the next morning with his hair a mess and his eyes bloodshot.

One of the cowboys says, "Man, what happened to you?"

"Daryl snored so loudly that I just sat up and watched him all night."

The next night it is a different cowboy's turn. In the morning, the same thing happens—the cowboy's hair is standing up, eyes bloodshot.

The other cowboys say, "Man, what happened to you? You look awful!"

He replies, "Man, that Daryl! Shakes the roof. I watched him all night."

The third night is Frank's turn. Frank is a big burly ex-football player—a man's man. The next morning he comes to breakfast bright eyed and bushy tailed.

"Good morning!" he says.

The cowboys can't believe it! They say, "Man, what happened?"

Frank says, "Well, we got ready for bed. I went and tucked Daryl into bed and kissed him goodnight. He sat up and watched me all night long."

Working on the Ranch

At the end of a workday, one cowboy tells another, "That new bull nearly did me in today, pardner."

"Oh yeah, what happened?" asks the other cowboy.

"I was putting out the feed when the sucker came charging at me like a locomotive from hell. He damn near got me!" replies the first cowboy.

"So, how'd you get away?"

"Well, the bull kept slipping. He slipped three times, and that gave me a chance to make it to the fence and jump over," replies the first cowboy.

"Man, that's scary! If it'd been me, I would probably have crapped all over the place," remarks the second cowboy.

The first cowboy replies, "I did! What do you think that bull was slipping in?"

New on the Ranch

A rancher hires a new kid and introduces the young man to the other cowboys.

"Boys, this is my cousin from Oklahoma," says the boss. "Show him the ropes 'round here."

"Welcome, pardner," says one cowboy. "What should we call you?"

"Well, my real name is Clint, but people back home call me Dishwasher," says the new cowboy.

"Dishwasher? What kind of name is that?"

"I got that der name on account of once I woke up drunker than a hillbilly at a cockfight and mistook the cook's dishwater bucket for the lavatory. Ever since, I've been called Dishwasher."

Calf Lift

A traveling businessman comes across a ranch one day and finds a cowboy lifting a calf in his arms so that it can nibble an apple hanging from a tree.

"Sure takes a lot of time to feed a calf that way," cracks the businessman.

"Yep," replies the rancher, "but what's time to a calf?"

Raise

A cowboy is drinking at a bar all night after a week's hard work on the ranch when his boss suddenly comes in and tells him that he is giving him a raise of $10 a month.

"Th' heck!" says the cowboy. "I ain't even drunk up last month's pay yet. That extra 10 will kill me fer sure!"

Bar Purchase

After several years of working the ranches of Texas, two cowboy brothers save up enough money to quit the cowboy life for good and purchase the town's only saloon.

The townsfolk look on with curiosity as the two brothers appear to be fixing up the place for a grand re-opening. But after two weeks with no apparent progress, curiosity turns to anger when construction takes too long.

"When you goin' to open 'er up!?" screams a man in a crowd outside the saloon. "We needs a drink!"

The two brothers emerge from the saloon into the light of day, all bleary-eyed and ragged.

"Open?" answers one of the brothers. "We bought this joint for our own drinkin'."

Psychotherapist

A psychotherapist starts up a business in a small old Western town, and in order to attract new patients, he asks a young cowboy artist to design a sign to hang outside his office. But three weeks after the sign is put up, the psychotherapist is still waiting for his first patient. What seems odd to him is the number of women who approach the office then walk away suddenly. So he decides to look at the sign for the first time that the artist made. Because of shortage of space, the cowboy had put:

PSYCHO

THE

RAPIST

Weekend Revelry

A cowhand gets paid on Friday and immediately rides into town and heads to the nearest saloon to get thoroughly trashed.

A couple of the cowhand's pals decide to play a trick on him. They sneak out of the saloon, turn his horse around and go back to join their hapless friend for a few more rounds.

The next morning, when the ringing alarm clock and a glass of cold water in the face fails to have the slightest effect on the cowhand, his wife starts shaking him by the shoulders and screaming, "Tex, get up! You have to hit the goddamn trail, you've got work to do."

"Can't," mumbled Tex. "Too beat. Too tired. Can't even lift my head."

"Get the hell up!" she screams in his ear. "I've seen you this hungover 1000 times."

"Last night was different," says the wretched cowboy. "Some son of a bitch cut my horse's head off, and I had to pull him all the way home with my finger in his windpipe!"

Religious Work

A missionary in the Old West has spent weeks living with a tribe of Indians and decides to teach them English. One day, he takes the chief for a walk in the forest. He points to a tree and says to the chief, "This is a tree."

The chief grunts, "Tree."

The missionary is pleased with the response.

They walk a little farther, and the padre points to a rock and says, "This is a rock."

Hearing this, the chief looks at the object and grunts, "Rock."

The padre is really getting enthusiastic about the results when he hears a rustling in the bushes.

As he peeks over the top, the padre sees a couple in the midst of heavy sexual activity. He is really flustered and quickly says, "Riding a bike."

The chief looks at the couple briefly, pulls out his bow and arrow and kills them.

The padre goes ballistic and yells at the chief, "How can you just kill these people in cold blood that way?!"

The chief replies, "My bike."

Day Off

"Do you believe in life after death?" a rancher asks one of his new cowhands.

"Yes, sir," the new recruit replies.

"Well, then, that makes everything just fine," says the boss. "Because after you left early yesterday to go to your grandmother's funeral, she stopped in to see you."

Hard Work

A dumb country boy has been out fishing all day. It is hard work in the midday sun but he catches a couple of fish. Later that afternoon, he is walking down the street carrying the fish in a brown paper bag when he runs into one of his friends.

It was so windy in Calgary one time that a hen sitting against the wind laid the same egg five times!

"Hey! What you got in that bag?" asks his friend.

The boy tells his friend that he has some fish in the bag.

His friend says, "Well, I'll make you a bet. If I can guess how many fish you have in the bag, you have to give me one."

The boy says, "I'll tell you what. If you tell me how many fish I have in this bag, I'll give you both of them."

Oldest Profession

Two prostitutes are riding around town in their horse-drawn buggy during the Gold Rush in California. A sign on top of their buggy says, "Two Prostitutes…$50." A sheriff, seeing the sign, stops the women and tells them they have to remove the sign or they will go to jail. Just at that moment, another buggy passes by with a sign saying, "Jesus Saves."

One of the prostitutes asks the sheriff why he let the other buggy go, and he replies, "Well, that's a little different—the sign pertains to religion." So the two women remove their sign and ride off.

The next day, the sheriff notices the two women riding around again with a large sign on their buggy. Figuring he has an easy bust, he catches up with the buggy and sees a new sign, which reads, "Two Angels Seeking Peter...$50."

Hooky

A cowboy decides to take off early from his duties on the ranch and goes drinking. He stays until the bar closes and then heads home, at which time he is extremely drunk.

When he enters his house, he doesn't want to wake his wife, so he takes off his shoes and starts tip-toeing up the stairs. Halfway up the stairs, he falls over backward and lands flat on his rear-end. That isn't so bad, except that he has a couple of empty beer bottles in his back pockets, and they break, and the broken glass carves up his buttocks terribly. But he is so drunk that he doesn't know he is hurt.

A few minutes later, as he is undressing, he notices blood, so he checks himself out in the mirror, and, sure enough, his behind is cut up something awful. He repairs the damage as best he can under the circumstances and goes to sleep.

The next morning, his head hurts, and so does his rear, and he hunkers under the covers trying to think up some good story to tell his wife, when she comes into the bedroom.

"Well, you really tied one on last night," she says. "Where'd you go?"

"I worked late," he says, "and I stopped off for a couple of beers."

"A couple of beers? That's a laugh," she replies. "You got plastered last night. Where the heck did you go?"

"What makes you so sure I got drunk last night, anyway?"

"Well," she replies, "my first big clue was when I got up this morning and found a bunch of Band-aids stuck to the mirror."

CHAPTER TEN

Mixed Bag

The Amazing Texan

A traveling salesman visiting a small town in Texas sees a circus banner: "Don't Miss the Amazing Texan." The salesman is curious, so he buys a ticket and goes into the circus tent.

Suddenly, trumpets blare, the lights come up and all eyes turn to the center ring. The light shines on a table with three walnuts on it. Standing next to the table is an old-timer cowboy.

The old cowboy unzips his jeans, whips out his penis and smashes all three walnuts with three mighty swings! The crowd erupts in applause, and the elderly Texan is carried off on their shoulders.

Ten years later, the salesman visits the same little town, and he sees a faded sign for the same circus and the same banner: "Don't Miss the Amazing Texan." The salesman can't believe the old guy is still alive, much less still doing his act. So the salesman buys a ticket.

Again, the center ring is illuminated, with the table and the old cowboy as years before. But this time, instead of walnuts, three coconuts are on the table.

The old guy suddenly unzips his fly, whips his penis out and smashes the coconuts with three swings. The crowd goes wild!

Flabbergasted, the salesman requests a meeting with the cowboy after the show.

"You're incredible," he tells the old Texan, "but I have to know something. You're older now, so why in the world would you switch from walnuts to coconuts?"

"Well," replies the old cowboy, "my eyes ain't what they used to be."

Top Ten Old West Phrases That Will Never Sound the Same After the Movie *Brokeback Mountain:*

10. "I'm gonna pump you fulla lead!"
9. "Give me a stiff one, barkeep!"
8. "Don't fret—I've been in tight spots before."
7. "Howdy, pardner."
6. "You stay here while I sneak around from behind."
5. Two words: "Saddle Sore."
4. "Hold it right there! Now, move your hand, reeeal slow-like."
3. "Let's mount up!"
2. "Nice spread ya got there!"
1. "Ride 'em, cowboy!"

Bowl of Chili

A hungry young cowboy walks into a seedy cafe in Sante Fe, New Mexico. He sits at the counter and notices an old cowboy with his arms folded staring blankly at a full bowl of chili.

After 15 minutes of the man just sitting there staring at the bowl, the young cowboy bravely asks the old cowpoke, "If you ain't gonna eat that, mind if I do?"

The older cowboy slowly turns his head toward the young wrangler and says, "Nah, go ahead."

Eagerly, the young cowboy reaches over and slides the bowl over to his place and starts spooning the chili in with delight. He is almost down to the bottom of the bowl when he notices a dead mouse in the chili.

The sight is shocking to the young cowboy, and he immediately barfs up the chili into the bowl.

The old cowboy quietly says, "Yep, that's as far as I got, too."

Dream

An old man is riding in a stagecoach. Suddenly, a cowboy riding a horse pulls up to the left side of the stagecoach, and a riderless horse pulls up on the right.

The cowboy leans down, pulls open the stagecoach door and jumps off his horse into the stagecoach. Then he opens the door on the other side and jumps onto the other horse.

Just before he rides off, the old man yells out, "What was all that about?"

The cowboy replies, "Nothing. It's just a stage I'm going through."

Country Flea

A flea dies and goes to heaven. St. Peter meets it at the gate and they discuss how the flea would like to spend the rest of eternity.

SP: "Have you thought about it? Do you know how you'd like to spend the rest of eternity?"

Flea: "Yes, St. Peter, I have thought about it. I'd like to spend the rest of eternity on the back of a rich lady's dog."

SP: "So be it; let it be done."

A few weeks later, St. Peter wonders how the flea is doing so he checks up on him.

SP: "Flea, how are you doing?"

Flea: "Oh, St. Peter, I made a terrible mistake. This old broad washes her dog two to three times a day and she perfumes it. I'm nauseous, and I have a headache from the smell."

SP: "Well, you know that you don't get more than one choice on how to spend the rest of eternity, but you are supposed to be happy so I will give you another choice. Have you thought about what else you might like to do?"

Flea: "Oh yes, St. Peter! I have thought about it, and I'm sorry I didn't bring it up before, but I'd like to spend it in Willie Nelson's beard."

SP: "So be it; let it be done."

Out of curiosity, St. Peter checks on the flea a few weeks later.

SP: "Hello, flea, how are you doing now?"

Flea: "I'm sorry, St. Peter, I'm not doing well at all. I get shaken up in the middle of the night, get drenched with beer, hear foul language all the time and I get woozy with some sort of white powder that flies around. It's hell, St. Peter. I'm miserable!"

SP: "You know, flea, you're not supposed to change your mind about how you spend the rest of eternity, but it sounds like hell, so have you considered what else you might like to do?"

Flea: "Oh, St. Peter, yes! I have thought about it, and I want to spend the rest of eternity in Dolly Parton's bush."

SP: "So be it; let it be done."

Not being able to stand his curiosity, St. Peter checks on the flea again after a few weeks.

SP: "How's it going, flea?"

Flea: "Oh, hi, St. Peter. Well, it's kind of strange. You see, there was this big party. There was a lot of singing and dancing, I got bounced around a lot and there was this weird-smelling smoke in the air that made me dizzy. There were hands all over me, and I don't quite remember all that happened, but would you believe it? I'm back in Willie Nelson's beard!"

Q: What do you call a frog who wants to be a cowboy?

A: Hopalong Cassidy.

Down Under

A cowboy from a small town in Saskatchewan goes to Australia for a vacation where he meets an Aussie farmer.

The Aussie shows off his big wheat field, and the cowboy says, "Oh! We have wheat fields that are at least twice as large."

The two men walk around the Aussie's farm a little more, and the Aussie shows off his herd of cattle.

The cowboy immediately says, "We have cattle that are at least twice as large as your cows."

The conversation comes to a standstill until the cowboy sees a bunch of animals hopping through the field and asks, "And what are those?"

The Aussie, looking at the kangaroos and then at the cowboy with an incredulous look on his face, says, "Don't you have any grasshoppers in Saskatchewan?"

Powerful Stuff

A young country boy is sitting on the curb with a quart of turpentine and is shaking the bottle and watching all the bubbles.

A priest comes along and asks the boy what he is doing.

The little boy replies, "Well, I'm just shakin' the most powerful liquid in the world—it's called turpentine."

The priest says, "No, son, the most powerful liquid in the world is Holy Water. If you take some of this Holy Water and rub it on a pregnant woman's belly, she'll pass a healthy baby boy."

The little boy replies, "Shoot, that ain't nothin'. If ya take some of this here turpentine and rub it on a cat's ass, it'll pass a motorcycle!"

Name that Tune

One cowboy says to another, "Hey there, pardner. What the heck is that there rock that makes them words sound so much alike?"

"That's a rhyme stone, cowboy.

Top Ten Songs Cowboys Sing by the Fire

10. I Hate Every Bone in Her Body But Mine
9. I Ain't Never Gone to Bed with an Ugly Woman, But I Woke Up with a Few
8. If the Phone Don't Ring, You'll Know It's Me
7. I've Missed You, But My Aim's Improvin'
6. Wouldn't Take Her to a Dogfight 'Cuz I'm Scared She'd Win
5. I'm So Miserable without You It's Like You're Still Here
4. My Wife Ran Off with My Best Friend, and I Miss Him
3. She Took My Ring and Gave Me the Finger
2. She's Lookin' Better with Every Beer

And the number one country song is…

1. It's Hard to Kiss the Lips at Night that Chewed My Ass All Day

Chili Cook-off

Notes from an inexperienced chili taster named Frank, who is visiting Texas from the East Coast: "Recently I was honored to be selected as one of the three judges at a chili cook-off. The original judge called in sick at the last moment, and I happened to be standing at the judge's table asking directions to the beer wagon when the call came. The other two judges (native Texans) assured me that the chili wouldn't be all that spicy, and besides, they said I could have free beer during the tasting, so I accepted." Here are the scorecards and comments from the event:

Chili #1: Mike's Maniac Mobster Monster Chili

Judge One: A little too heavy on tomato. Amusing kick.

Judge Two: Nice, smooth tomato flavor. Very mild.

Frank: Holy cow! What the hell is this stuff? You could remove dried paint from your house. Took me two beers to put the flames out. I hope that's the worst one. These Texans are crazy.

Chili #2: Arthur's Afterburner Chili

Judge One: Smoky, with a hint of pork. Slight jalapeno tang.

Judge Two: Exciting BBQ flavor, needs more peppers to be taken seriously.

Frank: Keep this out of reach of children! I'm not sure what I'm supposed to taste besides pain. I had to wave off two people who wanted to give me the Heimlich maneuver. They had to rush in more beer when they saw the look on my face.

Chili #3: Fred's Famous Burn-Down-the-Barn Chili

Judge One: Excellent firehouse chili! Great kick. Needs more beans.

Judge Two: A beanless chili, a bit salty, good use of red peppers.

Frank: My nose feels like I have been snorting whiskey. Everyone knows the routine by now—get me more beer before I ignite. The barmaid pounded me on the back; now

> Two cowboys limp out of a zoo with their clothes torn to shreds. One turns to the other and says, "That lion dancing sure ain't as restful as they made out."

my backbone is in the front part of my chest. I'm getting wasted from all the beer.

Chili #4: Bubba's Black Magic

Judge One: Black-bean chili with almost no spice. Disappointing.

Judge Two: Hint of lime in the black beans. Good side dish for fish or other mild foods; not much of a chili.

Frank: I felt something scraping across my tongue but was unable to taste it—is it possible to burn out taste buds? Sally, the barmaid, was standing behind me with beer refills—that 300-pound bitty is starting to look hot, just like this nuclear waste I'm eating. Is chili an aphrodisiac?

Chili #5: Linda's Legal Lip Remover

Judge One: Meaty, strong chili. Cayenne peppers freshly ground, adding considerable kick. Very impressive.

Judge Two: Chili using shredded beef; could use more tomato. Must admit the cayenne peppers make a strong statement.

Frank: My ears are ringing, sweat is pouring off my forehead and I can no longer focus my eyes. I farted, and four people behind me needed paramedics. The contestant seemed offended when I told her that her chili gave me brain damage. Sally saved my tongue from bleeding by pouring beer directly on it from a pitcher. I wonder if I'm burning my lips off? It really makes me mad that the other judges asked me to stop screaming. Screw those cowboys!

Chili #6: Vera's Very Vegetarian Variety

Judge One: Thin, yet bold vegetarian variety chili. Good balance of spice and peppers.

Judge Two: The best yet. Aggressive use of peppers, onions and garlic. Superb.

Frank: My intestines are now a straight pipe filled with gaseous, sulfuric flames. I pooped in my pants when I farted, and I'm worried it will eat through the chair. No one seems inclined to stand behind me except that wench Sally—she must be kinkier than I thought. Can't feel my lips anymore. I need to wipe my butt with a snow cone!

Chili #7: Susan's Screaming Sensation Chili

Judge One: A mediocre chili with too much reliance on canned peppers.

Judge Two: Ho-hum; tastes as if the chef literally threw in a can of chili peppers at the last moment. I should note that I am worried about judge number three. He appears to be in a bit of distress as he is cursing uncontrollably.

Frank: You could explode a stick of dynamite in my mouth, and I wouldn't feel a damn thing. I've lost the sight in one eye, and the world sounds like it is made of rushing water. My shirt is covered with chili that slid unnoticed out of my mouth. My pants are full of lava-like poop to match my damn shirt. At least during the autopsy they'll know what killed me. I've decided to stop breathing; it's too painful. Screw it, I'm not getting any oxygen anyway.

> **Cowboy Wisdom**
> If you're ridin' a high horse, there ain't no way of gettin' down gracefully.

Chili #8: Helen's Mount Saint Chili

Judge One: A perfect ending. This is a nice blend chili, safe for all, not too bold but spicy enough to declare its existence.

Judge Two: This final entry is a good, balanced chili, neither mild nor hot. Sorry to see that most of it was lost when judge number three passed out, fell over and pulled the chili pot down on top of himself. Not sure if he's going to make it. Poor Yank. I wonder how he'd have reacted to a really hot chili?

Frank: (Editor's note: Judge #3 was unable to report.)

Translation

A Mexican bandit robs a Texas bank of $250,000 and escapes across the river. A month goes by, and the bandit thinks he is safe so he celebrates his good fortune at a local cantina.

A few hours later, a Texas Ranger walks into the cantina, sees the robber and drags him out into the dusty street. After he realizes he can't communicate with the Mexican, the ranger pokes his head back into the bar.

"Anybody here speak English?" he shouts.

"I do, señor," comes the reply.

"Then come here," the ranger orders. The conversation between ranger, translator and bandit starts.

"Did he rob the bank?"

"He did."

"Does he still have the $250,000?"

"Yes."

The ranger pulls out his Colt .45, holds the barrel of the gun to the bandit's head and cocks the trigger.

> **Cowboy Wisdom**
> It's better to keep your mouth shut an' look stupid than open it and prove it.

"Make sure he understands this next question real good," says the ranger to the translator. "Where's the money?"

In Spanish, the frightened bandit blurts out that the money is hidden in a waterproof bag at the bottom of the well in the town plaza.

The translator looks at the ranger and says, "He says 'I'm not afraid to die, you frickin' Gringo!'"

Good Trade

Jane is driving home from one of her business trips in northern Arizona when she sees a young cowgirl walking on the side of the road. As the trip is a long and quiet one, Jane stops the car and asks the young woman if she would like a ride. With a word or two of thanks, the cowgirl gets in the car.

After resuming the journey and a bit of small talk, the cowgirl notices a brown bag on the seat next to Jane. "What's in the bag?" asks the cowgirl.

Jane looks down at the brown bag and says, "It's a bottle of wine. Got it for my husband."

The young cowgirl is silent for a moment, and then says, "Good trade."

White Man Problems

A white government official says to Chief Two Eagles, "You have observed the white man for 90 years. You've seen his wars and his technological advances. You've seen his progress and the damage he has done."

The chief nods in agreement.

The official continues, "Considering all these events, in your opinion, where did the white man go wrong?"

The chief stares at the government official for over a minute and then calmly replies, "When white man find land, Indians running it—no taxes, no debt, plenty buffalo, plenty beaver, clean water. Women did all the work. Medicine man free. Indian man spend all day hunting and fishing and all night having sex."

Then the chief leans back and smiles. "Only white man dumb enough to think he could improve system like that."

Big John

A bar owner in the Old West has just hired a timid new bartender. The owner gives his new hire some instructions on running the place. He tells the timid man, "If you ever hear that Big John is coming to town, drop everything and run for the hills! He's the meanest, biggest, nastiest outlaw who ever lived!"

A few weeks pass uneventfully. But one afternoon, a local cowhand comes running through town yelling, "Big John is coming to town! Run for your lives!"

If you play country music backwards, your lover returns, your dog comes back and you cease to be an alcoholic.

Before the new bartender can exit the saloon to start running, he's knocked to the ground by several townspeople scurrying out of town. As he's picking himself up, he sees a large man approaching the saloon, probably about seven-feet tall, muscular, grunting and growling as he walks.

The big man stomps up to the door, orders the poor barkeep inside and demands, "I want a beer *now*!"

The big man pounds his heavy fist on the bar, splitting it in half. The bartender nervously pours a beer, his hands shaking, and hands it to the big man. The man roughly grabs the beer and downs it in one gulp.

As the poor timid bartender cowers behind the bar, the big man gets up to leave.

"Would you like another beer?" the bartender calls out.

"Dang it! I don't have time!" the big man yells. "I gotta get out of town! Didn't ya hear? Big John's a-comin'!"

Saloon

A cowboy walks into a saloon and orders 12 shots of tequila. The bartender watches as the guy downs one after another. As he gulps the 10th one, the bartender says, "I don't think you should be drinking those so fast."

"You would if you had what I have," the cowboy says, throwing back the 11th shot.

"Well, what is it you have?"

The man throws back his last shot and then says, "Fifty cents."

A Cowboy in the City

On a visit to Toronto, a cowboy is having a hard time adjusting to the crazy pace. So to get a little relief, he walks into the first bar he sees and orders a drink to relax himself. After sitting for a few minutes, he hears a voice say, "Nice hat." He looks around but doesn't see anybody near him. A few minutes pass, and he hears the same voice say, "Nice shirt."

He starts to look everywhere: behind him, up and down the bar, under his chair, behind the bar, everywhere he can think to look, but he doesn't see anyone. He starts to think the city is an evil place. About five minutes later, he hears, "Nice boots." The cowboy can't stand it anymore, so he calls the bartender over and tells him he has been hearing this voice.

The bartender says, "Oh that. That's the nuts—they're complimentary."

Jesus

A cowboy bumps into a drunk outside a bar. The drunk claims to be Jesus. The cowboy disagrees, but the drunk insists he is Jesus.

Finally, the cowboy says, "How can you prove it?"

The drunk says, "Come with me." They go inside the bar.

The bartender says, "Jesus Christ, not you again."

Toughest Man Alive

There was once an old-time cowboy who spent his life out in open country. He was tough, he had been mean and he survived through some difficult times that would have turned some men into babies. Now retired and living a simpler life, he allows himself some of the small pleasures in life. He decides to order up himself some of that fancy toilet paper from a mail-order catalog. He writes the company a letter, sends it off to New York City and waits for a reply. A few weeks later, he receives a letter that reads:

"Dear Sir,

Could you please look in your catalog and tell us the exact order number you require? We have many types of toilet paper for you to choose from.

Thank you."
Confused, the old man writes back:
"Dear Sir or Madam,
"I already used the catalog. Send me whatever.
Thank you kindly!"

Playing Politics

Judy Wallman, a professional genealogical researcher, discovers that Hillary Clinton's great-great uncle Remus Rodham was hanged for horse stealing and train robbery in Montana in 1889. The only known photograph of Remus shows him standing on the gallows. On the back of the picture is an inscription: "Remus Rodham, horse thief, sent to Montana Territorial Prison 1885, escaped 1887, robbed the Montana Flyer six times. Caught by Pinkerton detectives, convicted and hanged in 1889."

Judy e-mailed Hillary Clinton for comments. Hillary's staff of professional image adjusters sent back the following biographical sketch:

"Remus Rodham was a famous cowboy in the Montana Territory. His business empire grew to include acquisition of valuable equestrian assets and intimate dealings with the Montana railroad. Beginning in 1885, he devoted several years of his life to service at a government facility, finally taking leave to resume his dealings with the railroad. In 1887, he was a key player in a vital investigation run by the renowned Pinkerton Detective Agency. In 1889, Remus passed away during an important civic function held in his honor

> **Cowboy Wisdom**
> Water and truth are freshest at their source.

when the platform upon which he was standing collapsed."

Stagecoach

A stagecoach bounces down a rutted road, heading for Dallas. In the coach are a Texan, a very busty lady and a greenhorn from the East.

The greenhorn keeps eyeing the lady. Finally, he leans forward and says, "Lady, I'll give you $10 for a blowjob."

The Texan is appalled. He pulls out his pistol, shoots the greenhorn right between the eyes and shoves the body out the door.

The lady gasps and says, "Thank you, sir, for defending my honor!"

The Texan holsters his gun and says, "Your honor, hell! Just trying to keep down inflation. Around here, a blowjob goes for $2."

Ear to the Ground

The Lone Ranger is riding into town when he finds Tonto lying across the middle of the road with his head pressed closely against the ground.

The Lone Ranger reins in Silver and leans down to ask Tonto what the matter is.

"Stagecoach passed half-hour ago," says Tonto.

"How can you tell?" asks the Lone Ranger.

"Broke my neck."

Professor Rangers

The Lone Ranger and Tonto are riding their horses late one afternoon and they realize they're not going to make it home before dark. They find a suitable spot and make camp for the night. They pitch their tents, start a fire and commence cooking their supper.

As soon as they eat the meal and have cleaned up, they sit around the fire telling stories and singing songs. Soon, the sun has set and it gets dark. So they crawl into their sleeping bags and go to sleep.

Sometime in the middle of the night, Tonto wakes the Lone Ranger up. "Kemo Sabe, look at sky, what you see?" he asks.

The Lone Ranger replies, "I see a bunch of stars, why?"

Tonto asks, "What that tell you?"

The Lone Ranger pauses and thinks. After a few minutes, he says, "Well, theologically it tells me that God is powerful and great, and we're just small and insignificant. Astronomically, it tells me there are billions of stars up there, millions of galaxies and thousands of planets, some of which might have life on them. Meteorologically, it tells me we're going to have a beautiful day tomorrow. Astrologically, it tells me that Mars is in the constellation of Leo. Chronologically, it tells me it's about 2:30 in the morning. Why, Tonto? What does it tell you?"

Tonto replies, "Kemo Sabe, you dumber than buffalo chips. Someone stole tent."

Plane Trouble

An Englishman, Frenchman, Mexican and Texan are flying across the U.S. on a small plane when the pilot comes on the loudspeaker and says, "We're having mechanical problems, and the only way we can make it to the next airport is for you to open the door and jump—at least one of you might survive."

The four men open the door and look out below. The Englishman takes a deep breath and hollers, "God Save the Queen!" and jumps.

The Frenchman is really inspired by the Englishman's gesture and hollers, "Viva la France!" He also jumps from the plane.

This really pumps up the Texan so he hollers, "Remember the Alamo!" He grabs the Mexican and throws him out of the plane.

Watch the Last Step

A blind man is traveling by airplane to Dallas, Texas. On board the plane, he feels the seats and remarks how comfy and big they are. The cowboy sitting next to him says, "Well, sir, that's because everything is big in Texas."

Q: How do you catch a unique horse?
A: Unique up on it.

Q: How do you catch a tame horse?
A: Tame way!

When the plane lands in Texas, the blind man goes straight to a hotel bar in Dallas and orders himself a cold beer. The bartender serves him the beer, and when the blind man goes to pick it up, he notices just how large the mug is.

"Wow, this is a huge mug of beer," says the blind man.

"Everything is big in Texas," replies the bartender.

After three beers, though, the blind man needs to use the toilet, so he asks the bartender for directions. But the blind man gets lost, and instead of going to the bathroom, he falls into the hotel swimming pool.

As he flaps around in the water, he keeps screaming, "Don't flush! Don't flush!"

Moon Limerick

There once was a cowboy named Boone,
Who always hung out in a saloon.
He sat on a thistle,
And boy, did he whistle,
And he sat, picking them out by the moon.

Hot Dog and Beer

A cowboy walks into a bar and orders a hot dog and a beer. He downs the beer, puts the hot dog on his head, smashes it with his hand and walks out before the bartender can ask why he did that.

The next day, the cowboy returns and once again orders a hot dog and a beer. The bartender watches in amazement as the cowboy drinks the beer, puts the hot dog on his head and smashes it to pieces. Again, before the bartender has a chance to question him, the cowboy is gone.

The cowboy returns to the bar the next day and orders his usual, but this time the bartender says, "I'm sorry, we're out of hot dogs."

"Right," says the cowboy, "then give me a pack of chili-flavored potato chips and a beer."

So he downs the beer, puts the chips on his head, smashes them with his hand and heads for the door.

"Wait!" shouts the bartender. "Why did you smash the potato chips on your head?"

The cowboy replies, "Because you didn't have any hot dogs."

Wrong Place?

Back in the Old West, a well-dressed gentleman walks into a saloon in Colorado and takes a seat.

The bartender comes over and says, "What can I get ya, stranger?"

"Nothing, thank you," replies the man. "I tried alcohol once, but I didn't like the taste, and I haven't touched booze since."

The bartender is a little confused, but being friendly, he pulls out a cigar and offers it to the stranger.

But the man again refuses, saying, "I tried smoking once, didn't like it, and I have never smoked since. Look, I wouldn't be here at all if I wasn't meeting my son."

To which the bartender replies, "Your only child, I reckon?"

Survey Says

A census worker is assigned to cover a rural area in Montana. He asks a local, "Who is the oldest inhabitant of this town?"

"Well, now, we haven't got one. We did have, but he died three weeks ago!"

Drunk Argument

Two drunk cowboys are walking along.

One says to the other, "What a beautiful night—look at the moon."

The other drunk stops and looks at his drunk friend, "You're wrong. That's not the moon—that's the sun."

They start arguing for a while when they come upon another drunk walking, so they stop him.

"Sir, could you please help settle our argument? What's that thing is up in the sky that's shining. Is it the moon or the sun?"

The third drunk looks up at the sky and then looks at them and says, "Sorry, I don't live around here."

Tonto

Two guys are in a locker room when one guy notices the other guy has a cork in his ass.

He says, "How'd you get a cork stuck in your ass?"

The other guy says, "I was walking along the beach, and I tripped over a lamp. There was a puff of smoke, and a red-skinned man floated out. He says, 'I Tonto, Indian Genie. I grant-um one wish.' And I says, 'No shit.'"

Toilet Paper

An Indian walks into a trading post and asks for toilet paper. The clerk asks if he would like No Name, Charmin or White Cloud.

"White Cloud sounds like good Indian toilet paper," says the Indian. "How much is it?"

"One dollar a roll," the clerk replies.

"That seems pretty expensive," responds the Indian. "What about the others?"

"Charmin is $2 a roll, and No Name is 50 cents a roll."

The Indian doesn't have much money, so he opts for the No Name. Within a few hours, he is back at the trading post.

"I have a name for the No Name toilet paper," he announces to the clerk. "We shall call it John Wayne."

"Why?" asks the confused clerk.

"'Cuz it's rough and it's tough and it don't take no crap off anybody!"

Baby Boy

A Texan buys a round of drinks for everyone in the bar because his wife had just delivered "a typical Texas baby" weighing 20 pounds.

Two weeks later, he returns to the bar. The bartender recognizes him and says, "Aren't you the father of the typical Texas baby boy that weighed 20 pounds at birth?"

"Yup, shor am!"

"How much does he weigh now?"

The proud father replies, "Ten pounds."

The bartender says, "Why? What happened? He weighed 20 pounds just a few weeks ago."

The proud Texas father says, "Jest had him circumcised!"

Wind Problem

An old Indian chief is suffering from gas, so he tells his son to go to the doctor on his behalf.

When the son gets there, he says to the doctor, "Big chief, no fart."

So the doctor gives him some tablets and tells him to come back in a week.

The next week, the son returns. "Big chief, no fart," he says again. The doctor sighs and gives him some stronger tablets, telling him to come back in a month.

A month later the son returns again and says, "Big chief, no fart."

Getting impatient, the doctor finally gives him some super-strength tablets and tells him to come back in a year.

One year later, the son goes to see the doctor and announces, "Big fart, no chief."

What Now?

A couple of cowboys are out riding their horses in the woods when one suddenly collapses and falls off his horse. His friend dials 911 on his cellphone and shouts to the operator, "Help me! My friend is dead! What should I do?"

Cowboy Wisdom
The only way to drive cattle fast is slowly.

The operator tries to calm him down. "Take it easy," she says. "The first thing to do is make sure he really is dead."

The operator hears the man put the phone down then hears a rifle shot.

The man picks up the phone again and says, "Okay, so now what?"

Shopping

A poor country pastor is livid when he confronts his wife with the receipt for a $250 dress she bought. "How could you do this!" he exclaims.

"I don't know," she wails. "I was standing in the store looking at the dress. Then I found myself trying it on. It was like the devil was whispering to me, 'Gee, you look great in that dress. You should buy it.'"

"Well," the pastor persisted, "you know how to deal with him! Just tell him, 'Get behind me, Satan!'"

"I did," replies his wife, "but then he said, 'It looks great from back here, too!'"

Hey, Joe!

A cowboy rides up to a saloon, goes inside and orders a drink.

He just about has the glass of whiskey to his lips when a guy runs into the saloon and yells, "Hey, Joe! Your house is burnin'!"

The man leaps up, runs out and jumps on his horse just as he thinks, "Hey, I don't have a house."

He goes back into the saloon, sits down and raises the glass to his lips again. Just then a man comes running up to the door and yells, "Hey, Joe! Your dad has died!"

So he leaps up, runs out, gets on his horse and starts to head down the street when he thinks, "Wait a minute…my dad died years ago."

He goes back to the bar, and sure enough, he's just about to take a sip of his whiskey when another guy enters the saloon and says, "Joe! Congratulations! You've won the lottery! There's a pile of money waiting for you down at the post office!"

The cowboy gets up, leaps on his horse and starts flying toward the post office. He is almost there when he thinks, "Hey, wait a minute. My name ain't Joe…"

What's in a Name?

A little Indian boy goes to his mother one day with a puzzled look on his face.

"Say, Mom, why is my older brother named 'Mighty Storm'?"

"Because he was conceived during a mighty storm."

"Why is my sister named 'Cornflower'?"

"Well, your father and I were in a cornfield when we made her."

"And why is my other sister called 'Moonchild'?"

"We were watching the full moon while she was conceived. Tell me, Torn Rubber, why are you so curious?"

Another Drunk Cowboy

A drunk cowboy walks into a bar and says to the bartender, "Bartender, buy everyone in the house a drink, pour yourself one and give me the bill."

So the bartender does just that and hands the man a bill for $57. The drunk says, "I haven't got it."

The bartender slaps the guy around a few times then throws him out into the street.

The next day, the same drunk walks into the bar and once again says, "Bartender, buy everyone in the house a drink, pour yourself one and give me the bill."

The bartender looks at the guy and figures to himself that the man can't possibly be stupid enough to pull the same trick twice, so he gives him the benefit of the doubt, pours a round of drinks for the house, has a drink himself and hands the drunk a bill for $67.

The drunk says, "I haven't got it."

The bartender can't believe it. He picks the guy up, beats the living daylights out of him then throws him out into the street.

The next day the same drunk walks back into the same bar and says, "Bartender, buy everyone in the house a drink and give me the bill."

In disgust, the bartender says, "What, no drink for me this time?"

The drunk replies, "You? No way! You get too violent when you drink."

Baseball Game

A cowboy is at a baseball game for the first time in his life so he sits quietly in his seat. The first batter approaches the mound, takes a few swings and then hits a double. Everyone jumps to their feet screaming, "Run! Run!"

This happens two more times, with a single and a triple. The cowboy is now excited and ready to get into the game.

Q: Why did the cowboy die with his boots on?

A: Because he didn't want to stub his toe when he kicked the bucket!

The next batter comes up and lets four balls go by. The umpire calls, "Walk," and the batter starts on a slow trot to first. The cowboy, extremely excited now, stands up and screams, "R-R-Run ya basstarrd, rrrun!"

Everyone around him starts laughing. The cowboy, extremely embarrassed, sits back down. A friendly fan, seeing the cowboy's embarrassment, leans over and says, "He can't run—he got four balls."

The cowboy then stands up and screams, "Walk with pride, man…walk with pride!"

Coincidence

A rancher goes into a local tavern and takes a seat at the bar next to a woman patron and orders a glass of champagne.

The woman perks up and says, "How about that? I just ordered a glass of champagne, too!"

He turns to her and says, "What a coincidence. This is a special day for me; I'm celebrating."

"This is a special day for me, too, and I'm also celebrating!" says the woman.

"What a coincidence," says the man. They clink their glasses, and he says, "What are you celebrating?"

"My husband and I have been trying to have a child. Today, my gynecologist told me I'm pregnant!"

"What a coincidence," says the man. "I'm a rancher, but I also have a few chickens. For years, all the hens were infertile, but today they're finally fertile."

"That's great!" says the woman. "How did your chickens become fertile?"

"I switched cocks," he replies.

"What a coincidence," she says.

Fishin' for Answers

A cowboy and his young son go fishing one day. While they are out on the water in their boat, the boy suddenly is curious about things in general and starts asking all sorts of questions.

He asks his father, "Why does the boat float?"

The father replies, "Don't rightly know, son."

A little later, the boy looks at his father and says, "How do fish breathe underwater?"

Once again, the father replies, "Don't rightly know, son."

A little later, the boy asks his father, "Why is the sky blue?"

Again, the father replies, "Don't rightly know, son."

Finally, the boy asks his father, "Dad, do you mind my asking you all of these questions?"

The father replies, "Of course not, son. If you don't ask questions, you never learn nothin'."

Visiting the Farm

A family from Vancouver is visiting relatives on a farm in Alberta. The family's young son wants to go hunting so the farmer lends the boy his gun, telling him not to kill any farm animals.

The city boy heads off and soon after sees a small animal. He manages to creep into range of the animal, which happens to be a goat, and shoots it. Not knowing anything about animals, the boy doesn't know what he killed so he runs to the farmhouse and describes the animal to the farmer.

"It had two saggy tits, a beard, a hard head and it stunk like hell!" says the boy.

"Oh, shit!" says the farmer. "You've shot the wife!"

Alien Visits Cowboy Country

Two aliens land in the Arizona desert near an abandoned gas station.

They approach one of the gas pumps, and one alien says to it, "Greetings, earthling. We come in peace. Take us to your leader."

The gas pump, of course, does not respond. The alien repeats the greeting but still gets no response. Annoyed by what he perceives as the gas pump's haughty attitude, the alien draws his ray gun and says impatiently, "Greetings, earthling. We come in peace. How dare you ignore us this way! Take us to your leader, or I will fire!"

The other alien shouts to his comrade, "No, you must not anger him..." but before he can finish his warning, the first alien fires at the gas pump.

A huge explosion blows both of the aliens 200 yards into the desert, where they land in a heap. When they finally regain consciousness, the alien who fired the ray gun turns to his comrade and says, "What a ferocious creature. It nearly killed us. How did you know it was so dangerous?"

The other alien says, "If there's one thing I have learned in my travels through the galaxy, it's that if a guy has a penis he can wrap around himself twice and then stick in his own ear, don't screw with him."

Don't Mess with the Best

At school one day, a teacher is trying to approach the topic of the birds and the bees and asks her students if they have ever seen anything on TV that is related to sex education.

Mary raises her hand and says she saw a movie about women having babies.

"Great," says the teacher, "that's very important."

Then Judy raises her hand and tells the teacher she saw a TV show about people getting married.

"Well, that has to do with it too," says the teacher.

Then Johnny raises his hand and says he saw a Western where some Indians ride over a hill, and John Wayne shoots them all.

The teacher says, "Well, Johnny, that really doesn't have anything to do with sex education."

"Yes, it does," replies Johnny. "It taught those Indians not to screw with John Wayne."

The Baddest Man Ever

- "Clint Eastwood" isn't an anagram of "Old West action." "Old West action" is an anagram of "Clint Eastwood."

- Clint Eastwood doesn't sleep, he waits.

- Clint Eastwood is the reason no other real cowboys are around anymore.

Top Ten Reasons to Date a Cowboy

10. We can do it with our boots on.

9. We can ride bareback.

8. We look good in tight jeans.

7. We know the right speed to ride.

6. Everyone knows we can last at least eight seconds.

5. We can ride all day and night.

4. We can rope a girl in.

3. We can be romantic too.

2. We are willin' to fight over a woman if we have to.

1. We can Git 'er Done.

Willie Clement

Willie has worked on farms and ranches for as long as he can remember. He has broken horses, driven cattle and once he was even lassoed to be the cook. They say that the cook is the most important member of the crew on a cattle drive? Well, maybe not that time... Willie now has his own ranch and wouldn't have it any other way. Some of his favorite memories come from jawin' around the campfire.